NEW AGE

INTERNATIONAL WEBSTER'S THE BEGINNER'S ENGLISH DICTIONARY AND GUIDE TO USAGE

NEW AGE INTERNATIONAL PUBLISHERS

First Indian Sub-Continent Edition : 2010
by New Age International (P) Ltd., Publishers

Branches:

- 36, Malikarjuna Temple Street, Opp. ICWA, Basavanagudi, **Bangalore**-560 004. Tel.: (080) 26677815 Telefax: 26615247, E-mail: bangalore@newagepublishers.com
- 26, Damodaran Street, T. Nagar, **Chennai**-600 017. Tel.: (044) 24353401, Telefax: 24351463 E-mail: chennai@newagepublishers.com
- CC-39/1016, Carrier Station Road, Ernakulam South, **Cochin**-682 016. Tel.: (0484) 2377004, Telefax: 4051303. E-mail: cochin@newagepublishers.com
- Hemsen Complex, Mohd. Shah Road, Paltan Bazar, Near Starline Hotel, **Guwahati**-781 008. Tel.: (0361) 2513881. Telefax: 2543669, E-mail: guwahati@newagepublishers.com
- No. 105, 1st Floor, Madhiray Kaveri Tower, 3-2-19, Azam Jahi Road, Nimboliadda, **Hyderabad**-500 027. Tel.: (040) 24652456, Telefax: 24652457, E-mail:hyderabad@newagepublishers.com
- RDB Chambers (Formerly Lotus Cinema)106A, 1st Floor, S.N. Banerjee Road, **Kolkata**-700 014. Tel.: (033) 22273773, Telefax: 22275247, E-mail:kolkata@newagepublishers.com
- 16-A, Jopling Road, **Lucknow**-226 001. Tel.: (0522) 2209578, 4045297, Telefax: 2204098 E-mail: lucknow@newagepublishers.com
- 142C, Victor House, Ground Floor, N.M. Joshi Marg, Lower Parel, **Mumbai**-400 013. Tel.: (022) 24927869. Telefax: 24915415, E-mail: mumbai@newagepublishers.com
- 22, Golden House, Daryaganj, **New Delhi**-110 002. Tel.: (011) 23262370, 23262368, Telefax: 43551305. E-mail: sales@newagepublishers.com

ISBN:978- 81-224-2810-0
Price: Rs. 200.00
C-09-12-4243

Printed in India at Rakesh Press, Delhi

PUBLISHING FOR ONE WORLD
NEW AGE INTERNATIONAL (P) LIMITED, PUBLISHERS
4835/24, Ansari Road, Daryaganj, New Delhi - 110002
Visit us at **www.newagepublishers.com**

INTRODUCTION

This book will serve as a great help to those who are learning English. Over 2,900 words are defined by the use of examples; more than 800 of these are also displayed as full colour photographs and illustrations. You will find the word you are looking for explained in English. As an added help, irregular verb-forms and noun-plurals are included where necessary.

a

Ted has **a** toy.
I saw **a** bird.

able

My elder sister is **able** to play the piano.
She **can play** the piano.

about(1)

Jane told a story **about** the ship.

about(2)

It is **about** two o'clock.

above

Above means **over.**
Jack hung a picture **above** his desk.

absent

John was **absent** from school today.
John was **not at** school today.

A

accident

I spilled milk on the floor.
It was an **accident.**
It **did not happen on purpose.**

ache

The baby has a stomach **ache.**
The baby has a **pain** in his stomach.
The baby is **sick.**

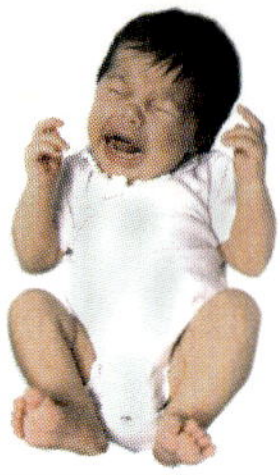

acorn

An **acorn** is the seed of an oak tree.

across

Jim threw the ball **across** the street.

He threw the ball to the **other side** of the street.

act

The teacher told the children to **act** well.

add

If you have one pencil and **add** one more pencil, you will have two pencils. To **add** is to **put together.**

This sign + means to **add** or **put together.**

address

Your **address** is where you live. Your house number, your street, your city and your state is your **address.**

admire

I **admire** the landscape.
I **like** the landscape.
The landscape is beautiful.

admission

Jack and Ted have got **admission** to the ball game.

advice

I made a house for my bird. My friend gave me some good **advice.** He **gave suggestion** to make it.

after(1)

The cat ran **after** the mouse.

after(2)

I came **after** you did.
I came **later** than you.

again

The girl rode the pony **again.**
The girl rode the pony **one more time.**

A

against

My bike leans **against** the tree.
My bike **touches** the tree.
We played **against** each other in the football game.
We played on **different sides** in the football game.

age

What is your **age? How old** are you?
How many years have you lived?

agree

Sam and Harry **agree.** Sam and Harry **think alike.**

ahead

The girl is **ahead** of the boy.
The girl is **in front** of the boy.

aim

Jimmy **aimed**
his arrow at the tree.
My **aim** is to be a doctor.

air

Air is what we breathe.
We cannot see **air** but when the wind blows we feel it.

airplane

We blow **air** into balloons.
An **airplane** is a machine that flies through the air.
There are many kinds of **airplanes.**
This is one kind of **airplane.**

airport

An **airport** is **a place where airplanes take off and land.**

alarm

A fire **alarm** makes a loud **noise.**
The **alarm** warns firemen
that there is a fire somewhere.
The bell on our **alarm**
clock rings to **signal**
us that it is time to get up.

alive

The car hit the dog but the dog is still **alive.**
The dog is **not dead.**

allow

My mother will **allow** me to watch television.
My mother will **let** me watch television.

A

almost

It is **almost** time to go to bed. It is **nearly** time to go to bed.

along

The boy is walking **along** the road.

already

Caroline has **already** learnt to play the flute.
Caroline has learnt to play the flute **before this time.**

also

Harry has a pair of skates.
I have a pair of skates **also.**

always

Mary is **always** good to her dog.
Mary is good to her dog **at all times.**
John **always** wins the race.
John wins the race **every time.**

among

Ted is **among** the boys going to school.
Ted is **in the group** of boys going to school.

ancient

The castle is **ancient.**
The castle is **very old.**

angry
angrier
angriest

I wanted to visit my friend. My mother would not let me go.
That is why I'm **angry.**

animal

Anything that lives and is not a plant is an **animal.**
A cow is an **animal.**
A fish is an **animal.**

annual

We are planning to have an **annual** school play.
We are planning to have a school play **each year.**
Annual means something that happens **every year.**

another

I drew a picture of the tree.
Freddie drew **another** picture of the tree.
I want **another** cookie.
I want a **different** cookie.

A

answer

My mother called Ann but she did not **answer.**
When the telephone rings, I will **answer** it.
I will pick it up and **reply.**

ant

An **ant** is an insect.

any

You may have **any** piece of candy in the box.
You may have **one piece of candy that you choose.**

apart

Tom sat **apart** from the other children.
Tom sat **away** from the other children.

ape

A chimpanzee is a kind of **ape.**

appear

At night the moon will **appear** in the sky.
At night the moon will **come out** in the sky.
When I turn the television on, a picture will **appear.**

apple

An **apple** is a kind of fruit.
An **apple** is good to eat.

April

April is the fourth month of the year.

apron

An **apron** is a piece of cloth worn in front to keep our clothes clean.

aquarium

I keep my fish in an **aquarium.**
I keep my fish in a **bowl of water.**

arm

Charles hurt his **arm.**
His **hand** hurts
from his shoulder to his fingers.

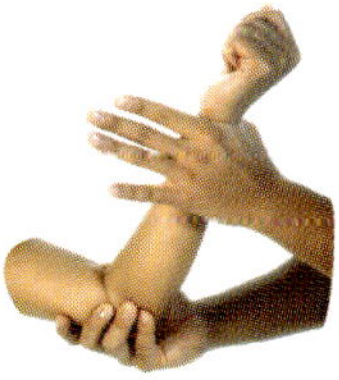

around

My father wears a tie **around** his neck.
He wears a tie that **circles** his neck.
The dog ran **around** the cat.

arrive

I **arrive** at school early every day.

art

Judy draws pictures in **art** class.
Painting and sculpture
are kinds of **art.**
Sewing, like music,
is an **art.**

ashamed

Yesterday I acted badly.
Afterwards I felt **ashamed.**

ask

When you want something from someone you **ask** for it.

asleep

The baby is **asleep** in her bed.
The baby is **not awake.**

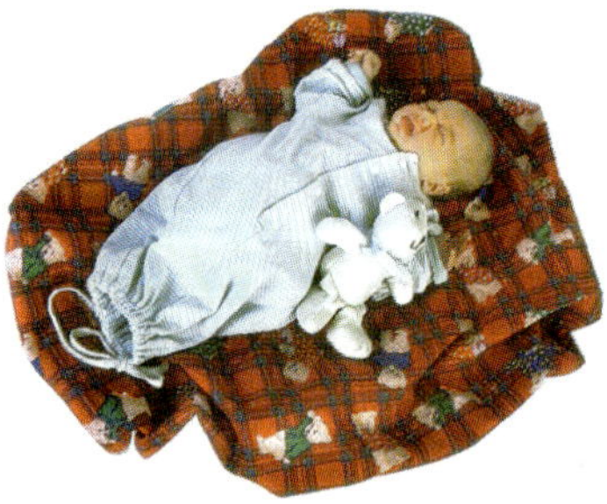

aunt

My mother's sister is my **aunt.**
My father's sister is my **aunt.**
My uncle's wife is my **aunt,** too.

autumn

A year is divided into four seasons. **Autumn** is the season between summer and winter. The leaves of some trees turn yellow and fall to the ground in **autumn.**

awake

The baby is **awake.**
The baby Is **not sleeping.**

axe
axes

An **axe** is used for cutting down trees.
This is an **axe.**

B

baby
babies

A **baby** is **a very young child.**
Our **baby** cannot walk yet.

---

bad
worse
worst

Fred is a **bad** boy.
He is **not a good** boy.
Something **bad** is **not good.**

---

bag

A **bag** is used to carry things in.
A **bag** is usually made of paper
or cloth.
Mother carried a hand**bag.**

---

bake

Mother put a cake in the oven to **bake.**
She put the cake in the oven to **cook.**

---

ball

The cat plays with the **ball.**
The **ball** will bounce and roll.

ballerina

A **ballerina** dances
in the ballet.
She **dances on her toes**
quite often.

balloon

Maria has a **balloon.**
She blew it up with air.
The air in the **balloon** keeps it inflated.

band

Harry plays music in a **band.**
Harry plays **the drums.**

bank

A **bank** is a place where we keep money.

bar

Cages are made with strong metal **bars** so that the animals cannot get out.

bare
barer
barest

When we go without
shoes and socks
our feet are **bare.**

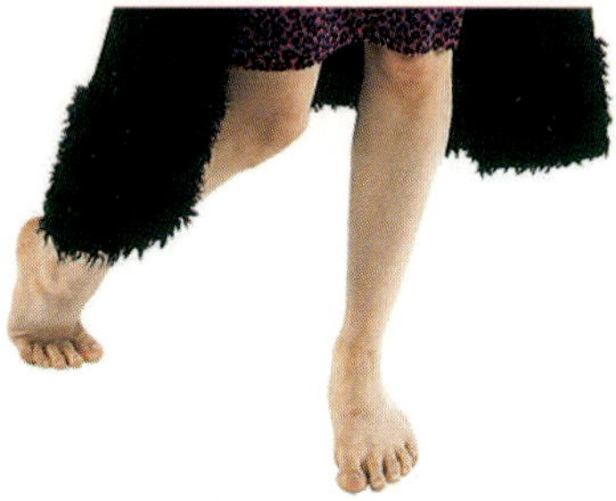

bark (1)

Our dog likes to **bark** at the cat.
He tries to scare the cat with his **barking.**

bark (2)

Bark is the covering of a tree trunk.

barn

A farmer keeps
his horses in a
barn.

barrel

We use a **barrel** to keep
food and other things in.
This is a **barrel.**

baseball

John likes to play **baseball.**
There are nine players in John's **baseball** team.

bat

A small animal that flies around at night is a **bat**. **The bat** looks like a mouse with wings.

bath

I help my mother to give my baby sister a **bath.**
We **bathe** the baby all over her body to keep her clean.

bathtub

The **bathtub** in which I take a bath.
Sometimes I take a toy boat into the **bathtub** with me.

beads

My mother has a string of **beads.**
A **bead** is a small, usually round piece of glass, wood or metal.

beans

Beans are a vegetable.
There are several kinds of **beans.**
Beans are good to eat.

bear

A **bear** is a large, shaggy animal with a short tail.
Bears are brown, black or white.

beat
beats
beating
beat
beaten

When I play the drum, I **beat** it with drumsticks.
When I play the drum, I **hit** it with drumsticks.

beautiful

The snow is **beautiful.**
The snow is **very nice** to look at. **Beautiful** music is very nice to hear.

bed

We sleep in a **bed.**

bee

A **bee** is a black and yellow bug that flies. **Bees** make honey.

beg

The teacher said, "I **beg** you to be quiet."
The teacher said, "I **ask** you to be quiet."

begin
begins
beginning
began
begun

Now let us **begin** to sing.
Now let us **start** to sing.

behind

Billy sits **behind** me at school.

believe

I do not **believe** it will rain.
I am not **sure** whether it will rain.

bell

The **bell** rings.
Some **bells** go "ding-dong."

belong

Whom does this coat **belong** to?
Who **owns** this coat?

belt

Tommy wears a **belt** to hold up his trousers.
He wears the **belt** around his waist.

bend
bends
bending
bent

I can **bend** a wire.
I can **bend** and touch the ground with my fingers.

beneath

The desk is **beneath** the lamp.
The desk is **below** the lamp.

berry
berries

A **berry** is a small, sweet fruit.

beside

Jane sat **beside** me.
She sat **next to** me.

between

Jill walks **between** her two friends.
She walks in the **middle**
with a friend on each side.

beyond

There is a mountain **beyond** the trees.
The mountain is **farther away** from the trees.

big
bigger
biggest

My elder brother is **big.**
My elder brother is **not small.**

bill

Father paid our food **bill.**

biography
biographies

Our teacher read the **biography** of George Washington.
Our teacher read the **life story** of George Washington.

bird

A **bird** has two wings, feathers and a beak.
There are many kinds of **birds.**

birthday

Today is Tommy's seventh **birthday.** Tommy was **born** seven years ago.

bite
bites
biting
bit
bitten

This dog will not **bite** you. This dog will not **cut** you **with his teeth.**

bitter

Mary took her medicine and it tasted **bitter.**

The medicine **did not taste sweet.**

blackboard

I like to write on the **blackboard** with chalk.
The **blackboard** is black.

blame

Do you **blame** me while you spilled the milk?
Do you **think it was my fault** that you spilled the milk?

blind

The man is **blind.**
The man **cannot see.**

blister

I burnt my finger and a **blister** appeared.
I burnt my finger and a **small swelling** appeared.

blizzard

The snow came down and the wind blew very hard.
We had a **blizzard.**
We had a **big snowstorm.**

block

I have a set of **blocks.**

blood

I cut my finger.
Blood came out.
Our heart makes **blood** move throughout the body.

blow
blows
blowing
blew
blown

I will **blow** the candles out.
I like to **blow** the whistle.
Sometimes I can hear
the wind **blow.**

blue

Blue is a colour.
Tom has a **blue** suit.
Tom also has a **blue** shirt.
The sky is **blue.**

board

A **board** is a piece of wood cut from a log.
We use wide **boards** to make a box.

boast

Some people like to **boast.**

boat

A **boat** floats on the water.
I like to ride on a **boat.**
A large **boat** is called a ship.

body
bodies

I try to keep a healthy **body.**
All the parts of a person or animal are its **body.**

B

bone

The dog likes to chew a **bone.** It keeps his teeth strong and healthy. We have **bones** throughout our bodies.

book

I like to read this **book.**
This **book** has pretty pictures and tells me about words.

boot

A **boot** is higher than a shoe.
A **boot** is usually made of rubber or leather.
I wear **boots** when it snows to keep my feet warm and dry.

born

The baby puppies were **born** today. The baby puppies were **brought into the world** today.

both

Lucy has lost **both** her mittens. Lucy has lost her **two** mittens.

bother

Ann lost her pencil.
She did not **bother** to look for it.

bottle

A **bottle** is usually made of glass and holds liquid.
Mother bought a big **bottle** of soda.

bottom

The lowest part of something is often called the **bottom.**
There is water at the **bottom** of the well.

bounce

I like to see the ball **bounce.**
I like to see the ball hit the ground and **jump back.**

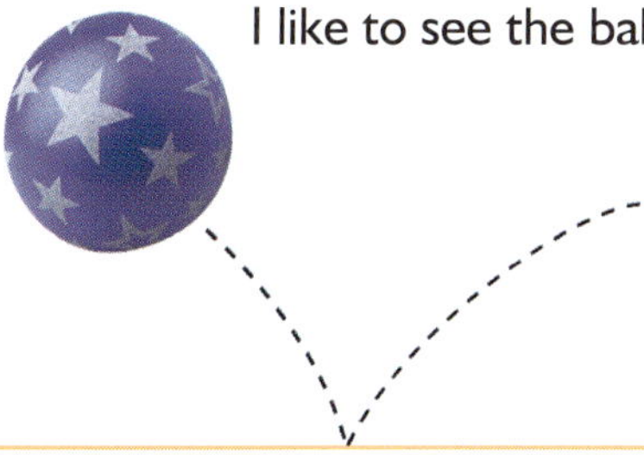

bow

Jack has a **bow** and an arrow.

bowl

The kitten eats in a **bowl.** I take soup from a **bowl.**
A **bowl** is a **deep, round dish.**

box
boxes

My breakfast cereal comes in a **box.**
My father's new hat was in a **box.**

boy

Frank is a **boy.**
He will grow up to be a man.
Frank's sister is a girl.
She will grow up to be a woman.

braggart

A **braggart** is a person who likes to brag.

brave
braver
bravest

The policeman is **brave.**
The policeman is **not afraid.**

bread

Bread usually comes in a loaf.
It is made of flour and other things.
A roll is **bread,** too.

break
breaks
breaking
broke
broken

Did you **break** the dish?

breath

Your **breath** is the air you take in and let out.

breathe

You should **breathe** through your nose.

breeze

A **breeze** is blowing through the trees.

bridge

A **bridge** is over the river.
We walk across a small **bridge.**
We ride across a large **bridge.**
Bridges are used to cross over something.

bright

I think Tommy is very **bright.**

bring

The postman will **bring** a mail to our house.
The postman will **come with** a mail to our house.

brook

We like fishing in the **brook.**
We like fishing in a **small stream of water.**

B

brother

John is Jane's **brother.**
They have the same mother and father. A boy that has the same parents as you do is your **brother.**
Jane is John's sister.

bucket

I filled the **bucket** with sand.
I filled the **pail** with sand.

bud

A **bud** is the beginning of a flower.
When the **bud** opens it will be a flower.

build

Jim is planning to **build** a house.
Jim is planning to **put together** a house.
Birds **build** nests.

bulb (1)

Mother planted a lily **bulb.**

bulb (2)

Before I read I turn on the light **bulb.**

bulldozer

A **bulldozer** is a tractor with a big blade in front which pushes dirt and other things.
This is a **bulldozer.**

bunch

I ate a **bunch** of grapes.

bunny
bunnies

We call a baby rabbit a **bunny.**

burn

I saw a house **burn** down.
If you touch a hot stove it will **burn** you.

bury

Dogs **bury** bones in the ground.
When we put something in the ground and cover it over with earth we **bury** something.

B

bus

A **bus** is larger than an automobile.
Many people ride in a **bus.**
I ride a school
bus to school.

bush
bushes

A **bush** has branches and leaves but is smaller than a tree.
Roses grow on a **bush.**

busy
busier
busiest

Mother is **busy.** She is at work. She is cooking dinner.

butter

Butter is made from cream.
Bread and **butter** are good to eat.

butterfly
butterflies

A **butterfly** is an insect.
It has four beautiful wings and a tiny body.

button

Can you **button** your coat?
Can you **fasten** your coat together with the **buttons?**

buy

When we go to the store we **buy** things.
We **give money** and **get something** for it.

buzzard

A **buzzard** is a large bird.
A **buzzard** is heavy and flies slowly.

buzz

The sound that a fly or bee makes is a **buzz.**

c

cage

A **cage** is a place to keep birds.

cake

My mother made a **cake.**

calf
calves

A **calf** is a male baby cow.

call

My name is William, but friends **call** me Bill.
I like to **call** my friends.
I like to **telephone** my friends.
Mother will **call,** "Bill, it is time to wake up."
Mother will **say loudly,** "Bill, it is time to wake up."

camp

We like to go to the woods and **camp** in a tent.
We like to go to the woods and **live** in a tent.

capable

My mother asked if I was **capable** of taking care of my baby sister.

can

I **can** tie my shoelaces.
I **am able** to tie my shoelaces.

candle

When I was one year old, there was one **candle** on my birthday cake. Now I am seven years old and there are seven **candles** on my birthday cake.

cane

The man has a sore leg and he walks with a **cane.**

canoe

A **canoe** is a **small, light boat.**
We move it with paddles or oars.

cap

The baseball player wears a **cap.**
The baseball player wears **a small hat.**

cape

I made a **cape** for my doll.
A **cape** is like a coat but it has no sleeves.
A **cape** fastens at the neck and hangs over the shoulders.

car

An automobile is a **car.**

card

My friend sent me a birthday **card.**
A **card** is a flat folded piece of stiff paper.

careful

Mother said, "Please be **careful** when you cross the street."
Mother said, "Please **pay attention** when you cross the street."

carry

When you **carry** something, you take it from one place to another.

case

We put things in a **case.**
A suit**case** is used to carry clothes in.

castle

The king and queen live in a **castle.**
The **castle** is a large building with thick walls.
It has many rooms.

cat

I call my **cat** "Tom."
Dogs chase **cats.**

catch

Ted can **catch** the ball.
He can **take hold of** the ball before it hits the ground.

cave

A **cave** is a large hole under the ground.
Sometimes a **cave** is called a cavern.
The bear sleeps all winter in a **cave.**

centre

There are two holes near the **centre** of the button.
There are two holes near the **middle** of the button.

certain

I like **certain** fruits but **some** fruits taste too sour.

chain

The prisoner was kept in a **chain.**

chair

A **chair** is something to sit on.

chalk

I like to write on the blackboard with **chalk.**

challenge

Bill is learning to ice skate because it is a **challenge.**
Bill is learning to ice skate because it is **hard to do.**

chance

There is a **chance** of rain today.

change

Mother asked me to **change** clothes.
She asked me to **put on different** clothes.

chase

The dog likes to **chase** the cat.
The dog likes to **run after** the cat.

cheap

Father bought a new hat.
The hat was **cheap.**
The hat **did not cost much money.**

check

The dentist **checks** my teeth.
The dentist **looks at** my teeth to be sure they are strong and healthy.

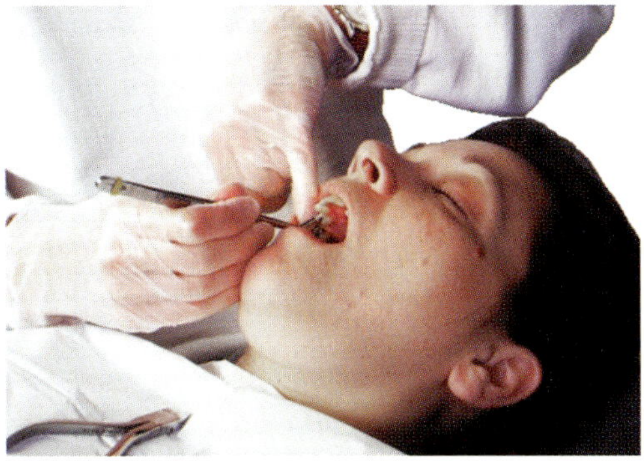

cheek

Mother kissed me on the **cheek.**

cheer

To **cheer** is to give a **happy shout.**
When our team won the ball game we gave a **cheer.**

cherry
cherries

My mother made a **cherry** pie.

chest (1)

Father keeps tools in his **chest.**
Father keeps tools in a **box with a lid** on it.

chest (2)

Your heart is in your **chest.**

chew

We must **chew** our food well.
The baby cannot **chew** because she has no teeth.

chicken

A **chicken** is a bird. A mother **chicken** is a **hen.**
A father **chicken** is a **rooster.**
A baby **chicken** is a **chick.**

chin

The **chin** is the lower part of my face.

china plate

Mother puts the **china plate** on the table.
Mother puts the dishes in the **china plate** on the table.

chip

There are chocolate **chips** in the cookies.
There are **small pieces** of chocolate in the cookies.

choose
chooses
choosing
chose
chosen

I must **choose** what I want to eat, an apple or a banana.

chop

The man used an axe to **chop** down the tree.
The man used an axe to **cut** down the tree.

circle

A **circle** is shaped like a ring.
We stand in a **circle** to play some games.

circus
circuses

The **circus** is a big show.
The children went to the **circus** and saw animals and clowns.
The **circus** was in a huge tent.

citizen

When a person lives in a country, that person is a **citizen** of the country.

city

I live in a **city.**
I live in a **large town** where people live and work.
The farmer lives in the country.

clap

When we like something, we **clap** our hands.
We **hit our hands together.**
Mary sang a song and we **clapped** our hands.

claw

A cat's **claw** is sharp.

clean

I help my mother to **clean** the house.
I help my mother to **get the dust and dirt out** of the house.
I **clean** my hands before I eat.

clear

The sky is **clear.**
There are **no clouds** in the sky.
The water is **clear.**
There is **no dirt** in the water.
I read the story but it was not **clear** to me.
I read the story but I did not **understand** it.

climb

See the cat **climb** the tree.
See the cat **go up** the tree.

clip

Mother will **clip** the dog's hair.
Mother will **cut** the dog's hair.

clock

I look at a **clock** to see what time it is.

close

I will **close** the door.

cloth

My dress is made of **cloth.** This is cotton **cloth** but there are other kinds of **cloth.**

cloud

The **cloud** is made up of tiny drops of water and dust.

C

clown

We saw a **clown** at the circus.
The **clown** was a very funny man.

club

A **club** is a heavy stick.

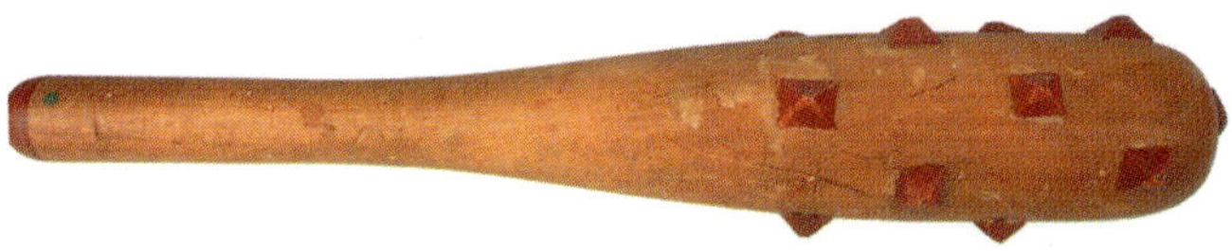

coal

Coal is a fuel.
Coal is hard and black and it will burn.

coast

The **seashore** is called the **coast.**
The **coast** is the land near the water.

coat

When I go outside,
I put on my **coat.**
The **coat** has sleeves and
keeps me warm.

cobbler

A **cobbler** is a person who mends shoes.

cold

It is **cold** in winter.
It is **not warm** in winter.

colt

The male baby horse is a **colt.**

comb

Jane's hair is tangled and she should **comb** it with her **comb.**

come
comes
coming
came
come

Bill will **come** to my party.
Bill will **arrive** at my party.

concentrate

The teacher said, "Please **concentrate** on your lesson."
The teacher said, "Please **think only about** your lesson."

cone

An ice cream **cone** is ice cream placed in a **cone-shaped** piece of pastry.

cook

Mother will **cook** our lunch.

cool

The weather is **cool** today.
The weather is **not warm** and it is **not very cold.**

copy

Can you **copy** this picture?
Can you **make a picture that looks the same?**
Please don't **copy** the way I dress. Please don't dress the **same** as I.

corn

Corn is a grain that grows on a corn cob.
Corn is good to eat.
When we grind grains of **corn,** we make **corn** meal.

corner

Bob waited for me at the **corner.**
Bob waited for me **where the two streets meet.**
Little Jack sat in a **corner.**
He sat **where two walls meet.**

cost

How much did the box of candy **cost?**
What was the **price** of the box of candy?

cottage

A **cottage** is
a small house.
We have a **cottage**
near the mountains.

cough

When I breathe smoke, it makes me **cough.**
I **cough** when I have a bad cold.

count

Bill can **count** up to ten.
Here are the numbers from one to ten:
1, 2, 3, 4, 5, 6, 7, 8, 9, 10.
I will help you. You can **count** on me.
I will help you. You can **rely** on me.

cover

Please **cover** the baby with
a blanket.
Please **put the blanket over**
the baby.

cow

We get milk from a **cow.**
Cow is a domestic animal.

crack

The dish has a **crack** in it.
The dish has a **small break** in it.

cradle

Baby sleeps in a **cradle.**
Baby sleeps in a **small bed**
that rocks back and forth.

crawl

The baby is learning to **crawl** on her hands and knees.
The baby is learning to **move on her hands and knees.**
She will learn to walk after she learns to **crawl.**

crayon

A **crayon** is made of coloured wax.
I like to colour pictures
with **crayons.**

cream

Cream is part of milk.
If we beat the **cream,** it will turn into butter.
Mother puts another kind of **cream** on her skin to keep it soft and pretty.

creep
creeps
creeping
crept
crept

Watch Baby **creep** on her hands and knees.
Watch Baby **crawl** on her hands and knees.

criticise

Bill asked the teacher to **criticise** his picture.
How dare you **criticise** your teacher?

cross

Mother said, "Do not **cross** the street."
Mother said, "Do not **go across** the street."

crown

The king wore a **crown** on his head.

cruel

The boy was **cruel** to his dog. The boy liked to see the dog suffer.
The boy was **not kind** to his dog.

crumbs

I fed the birds on some **crumbs** of bread.
I fed the birds on some **small pieces** of bread.

cry

When the baby gets hungry, she will **cry.** When the baby gets hungry, **tears will come** to her eyes and she will **yell.**
Mary is **crying** because her friends treated her badly.

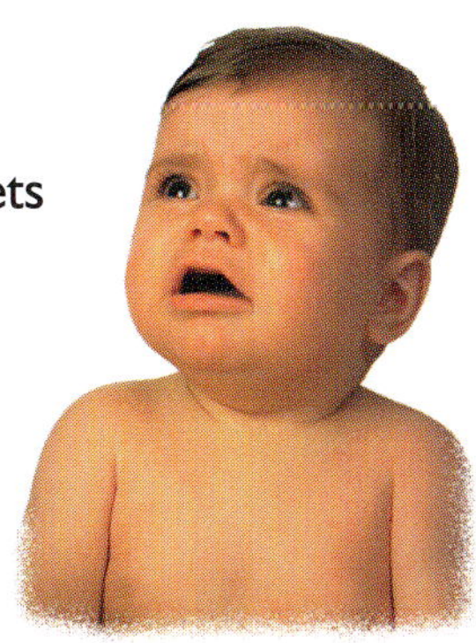

cup

The baby will drink her milk in a **cup.**

cure

Bob has a stomach ache but the doctor will **cure** it.

curl

Linda has **curls** in her hair.
Linda's hair is **not straight.**

curved

A **curved** line is not a straight line.
This is a straight line.

This is a **curved** line.

cushion

When mother watches T.V., she puts a **cushion** behind her back.
When mother watches T.V., she puts a **pillow** behind her back.

cut
cuts
cutting
cut
cut

Jim **cut** the apple with a knife.

cute

Our new puppy is **cute.**
Our new puppy is **little and pretty.**

dad

I call my father **Dad.**

dairy
dairies

We buy milk and butter at the **dairy.**

dance

The children like to **dance.**
They like to **move in time with the music.**

danger

If the light is red, do not cross the street.
The red light means **danger.**
The red light means **you may have an accident** if you cross it.

dare

Do you **dare** to jump across the stream?
Are you **brave enough** to jump across the stream?

dark

At night the sky is **dark.**
At night the sky is **not lit.**

dash

Mother called and I **dashed** home.
Mother called and I **hurried** home.

date

I look on the calendar
to see the
date of my birthday.
The calendar shows
the month, week and day
when I was born.

day

There are 24 hours in a **day.**
There are seven **days** in a week.
The first **day** of the week is Sunday.

decide

I must **decide** which dress to wear.
I must **make up my mind** which dress to wear.
I **decided** to wear the blue dress.

deep

The water in the pond is **deep.**
Deep means **how far in or down** something goes.

deer

The **deer** is a wild animal.
The **deer** eats grass and vegetables.
The father **deer** is called a buck.
The mother **deer** is called a doe.
The baby **deer** is called a fawn.

definite

The date of the party is **definite.**
The date of the party **has been set and will not be changed.**

delight

I will **delight** my sister with this gift.
She will be **happy** and it will give her **great joy.**

deliver

The milkman **delivers** milk to our house.
The milkman **brings** milk to our house.

demand

I **demand** from you to return my pencil.
I **ask you** to return my pencil.

den

The rabbit went to his **den.**
The rabbit went to his **home.**
A **den** is the home of a wild animal.

D

dentist

I go to the **dentist** twice a year.
The **dentist** is a doctor.
He keeps my teeth healthy.

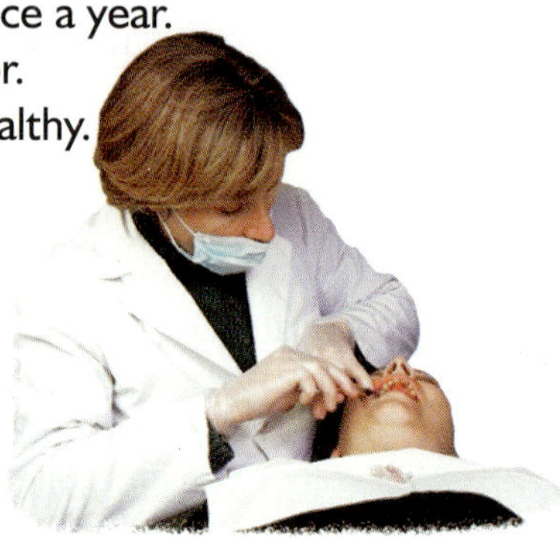

describe

Will you **describe** your vacation? Will you **tell about** your vacation?

desert

The **desert** is a large, sandy piece of land without trees and grass.
There is very little water and the sand is hot and dry in the **desert.**
Camels travel in the **desert.**

deserve

Mary helped her mother to clean the house.
She **deserves** a piece of candy.
She **should have** a piece of candy.

desk

A **desk** is a table on which we write, read and draw.
I have a **desk** at school.

destroy

To **destroy** something means to ruin something.
Please don't **destroy** the book.
Please don't **tear up** the book.

dew

The grass was covered with **dew** this morning.
The grass had **small drops of water** on it this morning.

diamond

Mother has a **diamond** ring.
The **diamond** is a beautiful stone.
It is clear as glass and it sparkles.

dictionary
dictionaries

A **dictionary** is a book that tells us the meanings of words.
This book is a **dictionary.**

die

The mouse may **die** soon if he gets caught in the mousetrap.
The mouse may **not live** any longer if he gets caught in the mousetrap.

different

The two balls are **different.** One is a baseball and the other is a football. **Different** means that they are **not the same.**

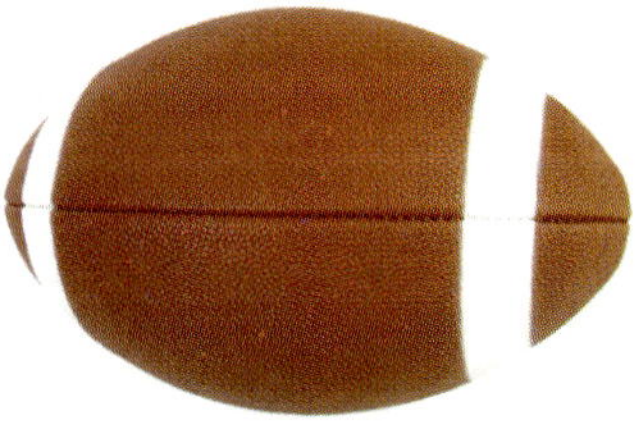

dimension

What are the **dimensions** of your house?
What is the **size** of your house?

direction

Which **direction** did the airplane go?
Did it go **North, South, East** or **West?**

dirt

Bill washed his hands to get the **dirt** off.
Bill washed his hands to get the **mud and dust** off.

dirty
dirtier
dirtiest

Bill washed his hands because they were **dirty.**
His hands were **not clean.**

disappear

The dog is eating his dinner.
Watch the food **disappear.**
Most of the food has been eaten.
Most of the food has **disappeared.**

distance

What is the **distance** from here to your house?

divide

When we **divide** a thing, we **make it into parts.**
I will **cut** the apple into three pieces.

doctor

A **doctor** is a person who takes care of your health.
When I am sick, Mother takes me to the **doctor.**

dog

John has a **dog.**
He feeds his **dog** every evening.

donkey

The **donkey** is an **animal** that looks like a small horse.
The **donkey** has long ears.

door

A **door** opens or shuts the entrance to a building or room.
I have a **door** on my clothes closet.

doorway

The **doorway** is where the door is.

dot

A **dot** is a small round spot.
At the end of this sentence is a **dot.**
We call this **dot** a point.

dreadful

The teacher said, "Your writing is **dreadful.**"
The teacher said, "Your writing is **very bad.**"

dresser

A **dresser** is a piece of furniture.
We keep clothes in a **dresser.**

drill

A **drill** is a tool.
A **drill** makes holes
in wood or metal.

drink
drinks
drinking
drank
drunk

When we **drink** we swallow a liquid.
Watch the baby **drink** her milk.
I **drank** my milk.

drive
drives
driving
drove
driven

My mother can **drive** the car.
My mother can **make the car go.**

dromedary
dromedaries

The **dromedary** is a **camel** that has one
hump on its back.
The **dromedary** is trained to run fast
and carry things on its back.

drop (1)

You may hold the kitten but you must not **drop** it.

drop (2)

A **drop** of rain fell on my nose.

drown

If you go into deep water you may **drown.**
If you are under water and cannot breathe,
you may **die.**

drum

A **drum** is a musical instrument.
We beat the **drum** with two sticks.
We beat some **drums** with our hands.

dry

When something is **dry,** it is **not wet.**
If it doesn't rain, the ground will become **dry.**
If it rains, the ground will be wet.

D

duck

A **duck** is a bird that can swim.
A **duck** has a wide bill and a short neck.

during

The teacher said, "Please do not chew gum **during** class."
The teacher said, "Please do not chew gum **while you are in** class."

dust

The wind blows **dust.**
The wind blows **tiny bits of dirt.**

dwarf

A **dwarf** is a very small person.

dwell

Where do you **dwell?**
Where do you **live?**

each

My father gave **each** of the children a toy.

eager

Ann is **eager** to open the box.
Ann **wants very much** to open the box.

eagle

The **eagle** is a large bird.

ear

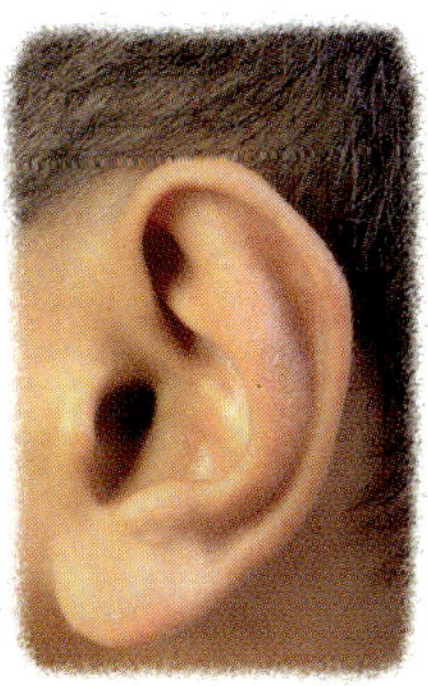

We have two **ears** to hear with.

early

I went to school **early** this morning.
Please come to my party and try to be **early.**

earn

Roy is a lawyer.
He **earns** a lot of money.

earth

Mother planted flower seeds in the **earth.**
It was hard to dig a hole in the **earth.**

East

The sun rises in the **East** and sets in the West.
When you face North the **East** is at your right.

easy

easier
easiest

The puzzle is **easy** to work out.
The puzzle is **not hard** to work out.

eat
eats
eating
ate
eaten

"Would you care for something to **eat?"**
"No, I have **eaten."**
"I **ate** before I came here."
After the baby awoke, she **ate**
cookies and drank milk.

eclipse

When the moon moves between
the sun and the earth an **eclipse** occurs.
The moon **blocks out the light from** the sun.

edge

The girl is standing at the water's **edge.**
She is standing where the water **ends.**

egg

I ate an **egg** for breakfast.
Chickens lay **eggs.**
Birds lay **eggs,** too.
A baby bird is born
from an **egg.**

eight

There are **eight** apples.
When you count them you say: 1, 2, 3, 4, 5, 6, 7, **8.**

either

Here are two books. You may read **either** of them.
You may read **one or the other.**

electric

Things that use electricity to work are called **electric.** The light bulb uses electricity.
Mother's **electric** iron uses electricity.

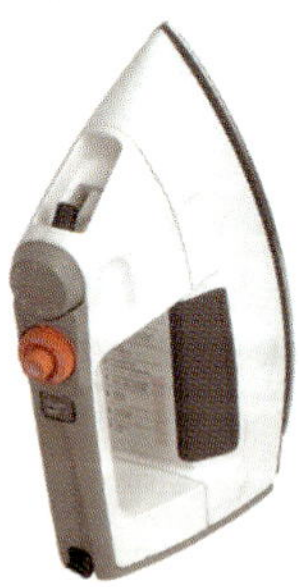

elephant

The **elephant** is a large, thick skinned hoofed animal.

elevator

We use the **elevator** to go up in the building. The **elevator lifts** us to the floor that we are going to.

empty
emptier
emptiest

The cookie jar is **empty.**
The cookie jar has **nothing in it.**

endeavour

I must **endeavour** to pass the test.
I must **try** to pass the test.

enemy
enemies

A soldier fights the **enemy.**
He fights the **people who are against him.**
You are not my **enemy.**
You do not **hate** me.

engine

The **engine** pulls the railroad cars.

enjoy

Did you **enjoy** the movie?
Did you **like** the movie?
Did the movie **make you happy?**

enough

Mary has **enough** cloth to make a doll's dress.
Mary **has as much** cloth **as is needed** to make a doll's dress.

envelope

When I write a letter, I put it in an **envelope.**
On the front of the **envelope** I write the name and address of the person to whom I am sending the letter.

escape

The bird cannot **escape** from the cage.
The bird cannot **get out** of the cage.

essential

Food and water are **essential** to stay alive.
We **must have** food and water to stay alive.

even

At the end of the football game the score was **even.**
At the end of the football game the score was **tied.**

evening

The **evening** is the time after sunset.
After the **evening** it is night.

every

I take a bath **every** day.
I take a bath **each** day.

everybody

Tom gave **everybody** a piece of candy.
Tom gave **everyone** a piece of candy.
Tom gave **each person** a piece of candy.

everything

The boys put **everything** in one pile.
The boys put **all the things** in one pile.

except

All the flowers **except** the blue one are red.
All the flowers **but** the blue one are red.

exchange

Mary's new dress is too large.
Mary's mother will **exchange** the dress for a smaller size.
She will go to the store and **swap** it for a smaller size.

excite

We were **excited** when the postman delivered a large box.
I get **excited** when I hear the fire truck.

excuse

Please **excuse** me for being late.
Please **pardon** me for being late.

exercise

We need to **exercise** to keep our body and mind healthy. When we run we **exercise** our legs.

exhausted

After playing football, I was **exhausted.**
After playing football, I was **very tired.**

expect

We **expect** that it will snow today.
We **think** it will snow today.

eye

We see with our **eyes.**
We have two **eyes** to see with.

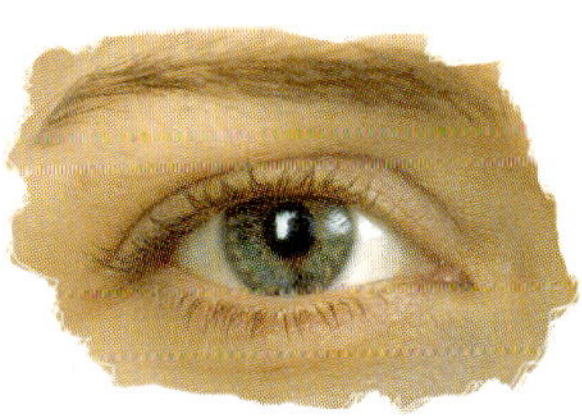

face

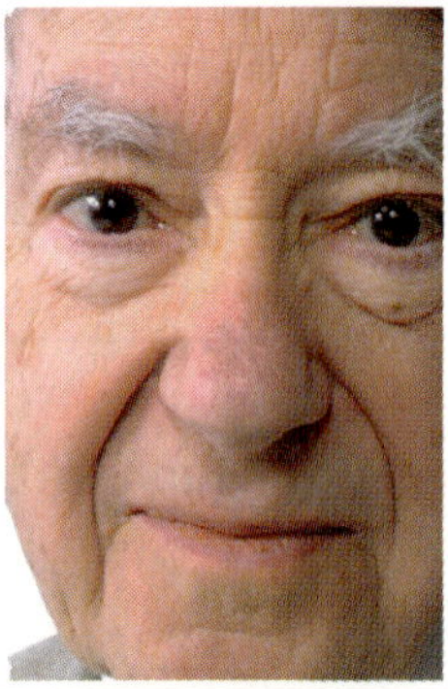

My **face** is the front part of my head.

fact

A **fact** is **something that is true.**
It is a **fact** that Tom has red hair.

factory
factories

A **factory** is **a building where things are made.**
Furniture is made in a **factory.**
Cars are made in a **factory.**

fade

Some clothes will **fade.**
Some clothes will **lose their colour.**

fail

Bill **failed** to hit the ball.
Bill **was not able** to hit the ball.

fair

We will play the game but you must play **fair.**

fairy
fairies

A **fairy** is a make-believe female person who can do magic tricks. We read about **fairies** in books.

fall
falls
falling
fell
fallen

Hold the baby's hand and don't let her **fall.**
The snow began to **fall.**
The leaves began to **come down.**

false

A **false** story is a story that is **not true.**

family
families

The mother, the father and their children make a **family.**

fan

We use a **fan** to keep us cool.
The **fan** moves air around the room.

far

The airplane is **far** away. The airplane is **not near.**

farm

A **farm** is a piece of land in the country. A **farm** is where our food is grown.

farmer

The **farmer** lives on a farm.
The **farmer** is the person who grows our food.

fat
fatter
fattest

The dog eats too much and he is **fat.**
The dog eats too much and he is **not thin.**

father

My **father** is my mother's husband.
I am the son of my **father** and mother.

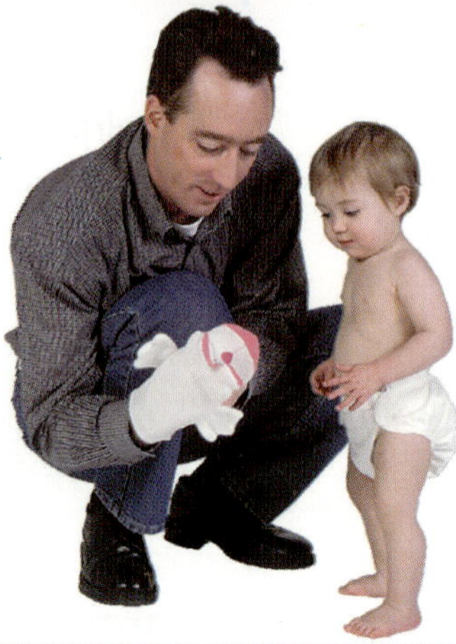

fatigue
fatigued

If you work or play too much, you will become **fatigued.**
If you work or play too much, you will become **very tired and weary.**
When you are **fatigued,** you are **exhausted.**

fault

The milk spilled but it was not my **fault.**

fear

I **fear** the dog when he barks at me.
I am **afraid** of the dog when he barks at me.

feather

A **feather** fell from the bird's wing. Some animals are covered with hair. Birds are covered with **feathers.**
Sometimes we say things are as light as a **feather.**

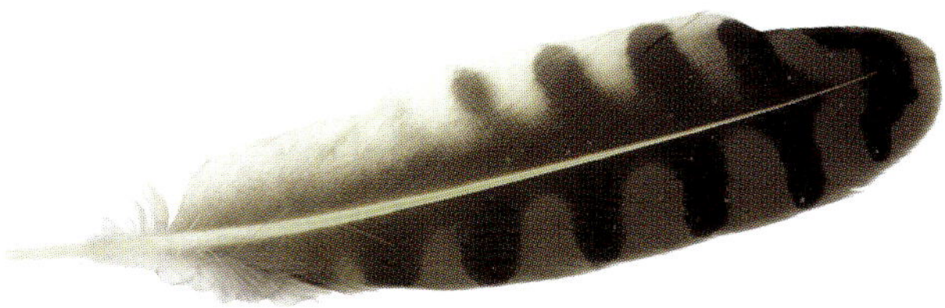

feed
feeds
feeding
fed
fed

I go to the pond and **feed** the fish.
I go to the pond and **give food to** the fish.

feel
feels
feeling
felt
felt

Would you like to **feel** how soft the kitten is?
Would you like to **touch** the kitten?

feet
foot

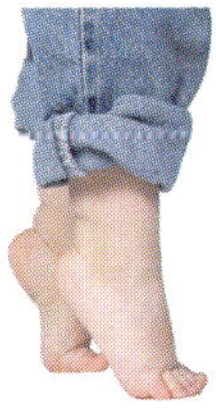

All of us have two **feet.**
We wear shoes on the **feet.**

feign

Mother said, "Don't lie in bed and **feign** sleep."
Mother said, "Don't lie in bed and **pretend** that you are asleep."

fellow

The young **fellow** doesn't feel well.
The young **boy** doesn't feel well.

fence

We have a **fence** around our yard.
Our dogs cannot get outside the **fence.**
This **fence** is made of wire but some **fences** are made of wood.

few

There are **few** flowers on this side of the hill.
There are **not many** flowers on this side of the hill.

field

A **field** is a flat piece of land.
Sometimes grass grows in a **field.**
Sometimes the farmer grows corn in a **farm.**

fierce

The tiger is a **fierce** animal.
The tiger is a **fearful** animal.

fictitious

Mother said that my story was **fictitious.**
Mother said that my story was **untrue.**
She knew that I had made up a **false** story.

file

We entered the classroom in a single **file.**
We entered the classroom in one **line,** each pupil behind the other.

fill

Fill the pool with water.
The man **filled** the pool with water.
The pool is **not empty.**

finally

I thought my dog was lost but he **finally** came home.
At last he came home.

find
finds
finding
found

Did Tom **find** his coat?
Did Tom **see** his coat?
Tom **found** his coat in the closet.

fine

I drew a **fine** line on the paper.
I drew a **thin** line on the paper.

finger

Mary has a ring on her **finger.**
We use our **fingers** to feel
and pick up things.

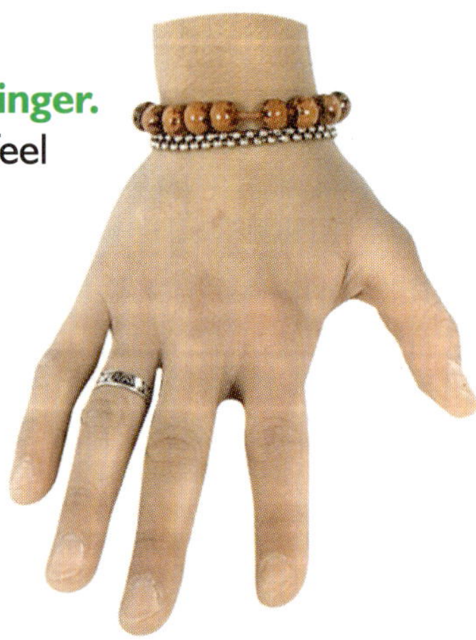

finish

Tom will **finish** his dinner soon.
Tom will **come to the end** of his dinner soon.
When Tom has **finished** his dinner, he will do his homework.

fire

Fire is hot and we must not get too near it.
Fire can be good or it can be bad.
We use **fire** to cook our food.
Sometimes **fire** can burn down a house.

fire alarm

We use a **fire alarm** to warn the fireman that there is a fire somewhere.

fireman

A **fireman** is a person who protects us from fires.
The **fireman** is trained to put out fires.

first

Jim got in to the school bus **first.**
Jim got in to the school bus **before anyone else.**
January is the **first** month of the year.

fish
fish

A **fish** is an animal that lives in the water.
Some **fishes** are good to eat.

fit

I will try the coat on to see if it **fits** me.
I will try the coat on to see if it is of the **right size.**

five

When we count **five,** we say: 1, 2, 3, 4, **5**.

fix

The toy is broken but I can **fix** it.
The toy is broken but I can **put it together** again.

flag

Each country has
a different **flag.**

flame

When fire burns, it makes a **flame.**

flamingo

A **flamingo** is a large bird that lives where the weather is warm.
The colour of the **flamingo** is reddish orange.
It has long legs and wades in the water.

flash

Watch the light on the pollce car **flash.**
Watch the light on the police car **go on and off.**

flat

The desk has a **flat** top.
The desk has an **even** top.

float

A boat will **float** on the water.
A boat will **stay on top of** the water. The boat will **not sink.**

floor

The **floor** is the bottom part of a room.
Mother puts wax on the **floor.**

flour

Flour is made from wheat.
Bread and cakes are made from **flour.**

flow

See the water **flow** over the dam.
See the water **run** over the dam.

flower

I gave a **flower** to my teacher. **Flowers** are pretty to look at and they smell nice. There are many different kinds of **flowers.**
A tulip is a **flower.** A rose is a **flower.**

fly (1)
flies
flying
flew
flown

Birds can **fly.**
Birds can **move their wings up and down and stay in the air.**

fly (2)
flies

A **fly** is a small insect with wings.
A **fly** is not clean.

fold

When I write a letter, I **fold** it.
I **bend** one half of the paper over the other.

foliage

In the autumn the **foliage** on the trees is beautiful.
In the autumn the **leaves** on the trees are beautiful.
The **foliage** turns bright red and orange.
The **leaves** turn bright red and orange.

follow

The dog likes to **follow** me.
The dog likes to **walk behind** me.

fond

Mary is **fond** of the cat.
Mary **likes** the cat.

food

We try to eat **food** that is good for us.
When we eat dinner, we eat **food.**

foot
feet

I have a left **foot** and a right **foot.**
My two **feet** are at the bottom of my legs.
There is a small house at the **foot** of the hill.
There is a small house at the **base** of the hill.

---

forehead

The **forehead** is the part of the head above the eyes and below the hair.

---

forest

The **forest** is where **many trees** grow.

---

forget
forgets
forgetting
forgot
forgotten

Did you **forget** to brush your teeth?
Did you **not remember** to brush your teeth?

---

forgive
forgives
forgiving
forgave
forgiven

Please **forgive** me for stepping on your foot.
Please **don't be angry with** me for stepping on your foot.

fork

We eat with a **fork.**

forward

If we move **forward**
we move **ahead.**
The teacher said,
"Take one step **forward.**"
The teacher said,
"Take one step **out in front.**"

four

There are **four** seasons in the year.
The **four** seasons are winter, spring, summer and autumn.

fox
foxes

A **fox** is an animal that looks like some dogs.
The **fox** has pointed ears and a bushy tail.

free(1)
freer
freest

Will you come to the show if it is **free?**
Will you come to the show if it **costs nothing?**

---

free(2)

Jane **freed** the bird. Jane set the bird **loose.**

---

freeze
freezes
freezing
froze
frozen

When the weather is very cold the water will **freeze.** When the water **freezes** it turns into ice.

---

fresh

This bread is very **fresh.**
This bread has **just been baked.**

Friday

Friday is a day of the week. **Friday** is the **day before Saturday.**

friend

Bob is my **friend.** A **friend** is a person that you like. A **friend** is a person that you can trust. Mary and Ann are **friends.**

frighten

The storm did not **frighten** me.
The storm did not **make** me **afraid.**

frog

The **frog** is a small animal that can jump very far. He has strong back legs. The **frog** can live in the water or outside the water.

fruit

I like to eat **fruit. Fruit** is healthy. There are many different kinds of **fruit.** Oranges, apples, grapes, peaches and cherries are **fruits.**

fry

Mother will **fry** the fish.
She will **cook** the fish **in a pan on top of the stove.**

function

How does the machine **function?** How does the machine **work?**

furnace

We have a **furnace** in our basement. The **furnace** is a **large stove** that keeps our house warm. Our **furnace** burns oil.
Some **furnaces** burn coal.

---

furniture

People have **furniture** in their houses.
Tables, chairs, beds and **lamps** are **furniture.**

gain

Tom will not **gain** anything by being rude.
Tom will not **get** anything by being rude.

game

Football is a **game.**
Baseball is a **game.**

garage

Father keeps the car in the **garage.**
The **garage** is a special room made just for the car.

garden

A **garden** is a **place where plants grow.**
We grow vegetables in a **garden.**

garland

A **garland** of flowers is a **ring** of flowers.
Judy made a **garland** of daisies and put it on her head.
Judy made a **ring** of daisies and put it on her head.
A **garland** is also called a **wreath.**

---

gasoline

The car must have **gasoline** to make it go.
Father buys **gasoline** at the **gasoline** station.

---

gather

Mary will **gather** some flowers for the teacher.

---

gentle

Judy has a **gentle** voice.
Judy has a **soft and kind** voice.

---

giant

A **giant** is large and strong.
The large, strong man in the story was a **giant.**
When a tree is **very large,** we sometimes call it a **giant.**

---

gift

Sean gave Tim a **gift.**
Sean gave Tim a **present.**

giraffe

The **giraffe** is an animal that has spots on his body.
The **giraffe** has long legs and a very long neck.
A **giraffe** can stand on the ground and eat leaves from tall trees.

girl

John is a boy and Mary is a **girl.**
When Mary grows up, she will be a woman.

give
gives
giving
gave
given

Would you **give** me one of your pencils?
Would you **let me have** one of your pencils?
The lady at the store **gave** me gum.
She **did not let me pay** for the gum.

glad

Jim is **glad** that his dog came home.
Jim is **happy** that his dog came home.

glass(1)

The window is made of **glass.**

glass(2)
glasses

We drink milk from a **glass.**

glove

A **glove** is worn on the hand.
The **gloves** keep our hands warm.

gnu

The **gnu** is a funny-looking animal that lives in Africa.
This is a **gnu.**

go(1)
goes
going
went
gone

Let's **go** for a walk down the road.

go(2)
goes
going
went
gone

What makes the car **go?**
What makes the car **work?**

goat

A **goat** is an animal that lives on the farm. The male **goat** has horns and a beard.

gold

Gold is a beautiful yellow **metal.**
Mother has a watch made of **gold.**
I have a **gold** ring.

good
better
best

I eat vegetables because they are **good** for me.
I eat vegetables because they help **make me healthy.**
Jane is a **good** girl. Jane is **not a bad** girl.

---

goose
geese

A **goose** is a large bird that can swim.
A **goose** looks like a duck but it has a longer neck.
A **goose** is good to eat.

---

gorilla

The **gorilla** is an animal that lives in Africa. The **gorilla** walks and moves almost like a person.

---

grade

Bob is in the first **grade** at school.

---

grain

My breakfast cereal is made from **grain.** My breakfast cereal is made from **corn.** Wheat is a **grain** and rice is a **grain** too.
A **tiny piece** of salt is a **grain** of salt.
A tiny piece of sand is called a **grain** of sand.

grandmother

Your mother's mother is your **grandmother.**
Your father's mother is your **grandmother** too.

grape

A **grape** is a fruit. A **grape** is red, purple or green.
Grapes grow in bunches on a vine.

grass

We have **grass** in our yard.
Grass is a **plant**
that covers our lawn.
Some animals eat **grass.**

great

The blue whale is a **great** animal.
The blue whale is the **biggest** animal in the world.

greedy

Please eat some pie but don't be **greedy.**
Please eat some pie but don't eat **more than your share.**

ground

The farmer puts seeds in the **ground.**
The farmer puts seeds in the **earth.**

group

The teacher asked the children to move into a **group.** The teacher asked the children to move **close together. Several people** or **things together** form a **group.**

grow
grows
growing
grew
grown

When you **grow,** you get larger.
The plant will **grow.**
The animal will **grow.**

guarantee

I **guarantee** that I will come to your party.
I **promise for sure** that I will come to your party.

guess(1)

Can you **guess** the number?
Can you **think** of the right number?

guess(2)

I **guess** you can do it.

guest

Bill was a **guest** at John's house.
Bill was a **visitor** at John's house.
We had **guests** for lunch.
We had **company** for lunch.

guide

Jane will **guide** you to Mary's house.
Jane will **show you the way** to Mary's house.

gum

The flesh around the base of my teeth is called a **gum.**

gust

A **gust** of wind blew Tom's cap from his head.
A sudden, strong rush of air is called a **gust.**

hair

Hair grows on a person's **head.**

half
halves

Jane broke the candy in **half.**
Jane broke the candy
in **two pieces.**
Each piece was of
the same size.

hand

We use our **hand** to pick up things.
We have two **hands.**
There are five **fingers** in each
hand.

handkerchief

I carry a **handkerchief** in my pocket.
The **handkerchief** is a piece of cloth.
I blow my nose in the **handkerchief.**

handle

The cup has a **handle.** This pan has a **handle.**
A **handle** is used for picking something up.

handsome

Mary's father is **handsome.**

hang
hangs
hanging
hung
hung

We **hang** our clothes in the closet.

happen

Did you see the accident **happen?**

happy
happier
happiest

The new bike made Tom **happy.**
The new bike made Tom **joyful.**
The new bike made Tom **very pleased.**

hard

Bill won the race but it was **hard** to do.
Bill won the race but it was **not easy** to do.
A rock is **hard.**
A rock is **not soft.**

hare

The **hare** is a rabbit.
The **hare** is larger than most rabbits.

harm

Please do not **harm** the cat.
Please do not **hurt** the cat.

harmony

The people live in **harmony.**
The people are **peaceful and friendly.**
The group sings in **harmony.**
The group sings **together.**

hatch

The hen sits on the eggs to **hatch** them.
In three weeks chicks will **come out of** the eggs.

hate

Do you **hate** me?
Do you **dislike** me **very much?**

have
has
having
had

I **have** a new radio.
I **own** a new radio.

H

hay

Hay is dried grass.
The farmer feeds **hay**
to the cows.

head

The **head** is **the top part of our body.**
The **head** is above our neck.
We have hair on the top of our **head.**
Bob is **head** in his class.
Bob is **first** in his class.

hear
hears
hearing
heard

Did you **hear** the music?
Did you **listen to** the music?
We **hear** with our ears.

heart

The **heart** moves blood through my body and keeps me healthy.
Mary lives in the **heart** of the city.
Mary lives in the **centre** of the city.

heat

Mother will **heat** the soup by putting it over the fire.
Mother will **make** the soup **hot** by putting it over the fire.

heavy
heavier
heaviest

The basket of apples is **heavy.**
The basket of apples is **hard to lift.**

heel(1)

Your **heel** is the back part of your foot.

heel(2)

The **heel** of your shoe is the raised part of the shoe.

help

I will **help** my mother to clean the house.

hemisphere

Half of our earth is a **hemisphere.**
We divide the earth into four **hemispheres.**
Northern, Southern, Eastern, and Western are the four **hemispheres.**

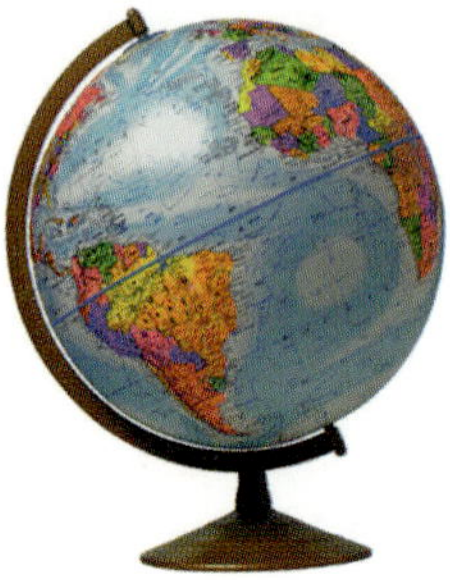

hen

The **hen** is a mother chicken.
The **hen** will lay eggs.

her

Her dress is pretty.

here

Please meet me **here** tomorrow.
Please meet me **at this place** tomorrow.

hide
hides
hiding
hid
hidden

The dog is digging a hole to **hide** his bone in.
The dog is digging a hole to **put** his bone **out of sight.**

high
high
higher
highest

The building is very **high.**

hill

Jack and Jill went up the **hill.**
The **hill** is **a piece of land that is higher than the land around it.**

his

Bill is riding **his** pony.
Bill **owns** the pony.

H

hit
hits
hitting
hit

Did the red car **hit** the blue car?
Did the red car **bump** into the blue car?

hive

The bees live in a **hive.**
The bees live in a small house which is called a bee**hive.**

hold
holds
holding
held

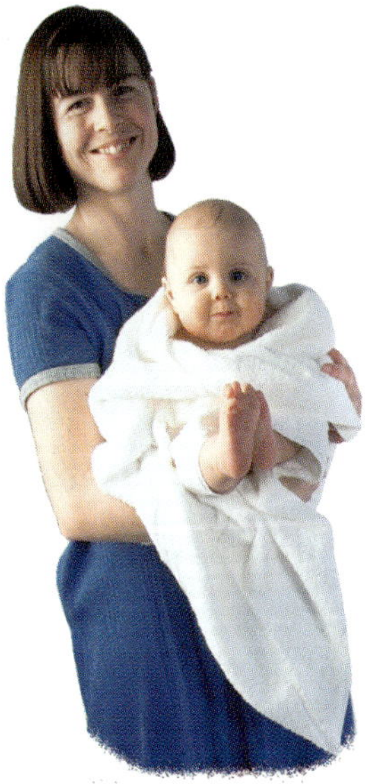

Would you **hold** the baby?
Would you **keep** the baby **in your hands and arms?**

hole

Bill has a **hole** in his shoe.
Bill has an **opening** in his shoe and he can see through it.

home

I must go **home** after school.
I must go to the **place where I live** after school.
The rabbit lives in a **den.**
The **den** is the lion's **home.**

honest

Mary is **honest.**
Mary **will not lie or steal.**
You can trust Mary.

hoop

Jim likes to roll the **hoop.**
The hoop is a **metal ring.**

hop

The frog can **hop** very far.

horn(1)

We make noise with a **horn.**
We blow into one end of the **horn** and the sound comes out of the other end.

horn(2)

The cow has **horns** on her head.

horse

A **horse** is an animal.
The **horse** is strong and can pull a wagon.
The **horse** can run very fast.
A cowboy rides on the back of a **horse.**
The children are riding a **horse.**

hose

Father uses a **hose** to water the lawn.
The **hose** is a long rubber tube and water passes through it.

hospital

We go to the **hospital** when we are sick.
The **hospital** is a building where doctors and nurses work.

hot
hotter
hottest

Don't touch the **hot** stove. It will burn you.

hour

One **hour** is sixty minutes.
One **hour** is when the big hand goes around the clock one time.
There are twenty-four **hours** in a day.

how

Please tell me **how** to get to your house.
The doctor said, **"How** do you feel?"

hug

Caroline gave her father a **hug.**
Caroline **put** her **arms around** her father and **held him tight.**

huge

The elephant is **huge.**
The elephant is **very large.**

hump

The camel has a **hump** on his back.

hungry
hungrier
hungriest

The baby is **hungry.**
The baby **wants**
to eat something.
When the baby's stomach
feels empty
she becomes **hungry.**

hurry

Mother said, "Please **hurry** home."
Mother said, "Please come home **as fast as you can."**

hurt
hurts
hurting
hurt

Did you **hurt** your leg?
Do you **feel pain** in your leg?
You must not **hurt** the dog.
You must not **harm** the dog.

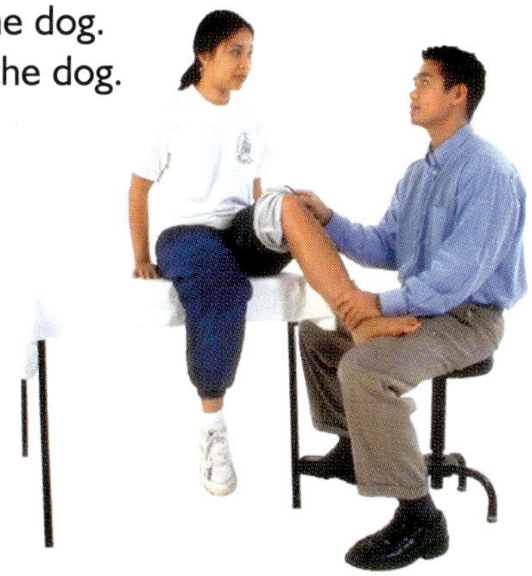

hush

The teacher told the class to **hush.**
The teacher told the class to **keep quiet.**

hydrant

When there is a fire the fireman connects the hose to the fire **hydrant.**
Water comes out of the **hydrant.**

ice

When water becomes very cold, it turns into **ice.**
We skate on the pond when the water freezes and turns into **ice.**

idea

I have the **idea** that the kitten is lost.
I **think** the kitten is lost.

identical

The two dolls are **identical.**
The two dolls look **the same.**
They are **exactly alike.**

igloo

The Eskimos live in an **igloo.**
The Eskimos live in **houses made of snow blocks.**
This is an **igloo.**

ill

Tom is **ill** today.

impolite

Jane was **impolite** to her brother.
Jane was **not polite** to her brother.
Jane was **rude** to her brother.

increase

When it rains the pond will **increase** in size. When it rains the pond will **become larger.** Please **increase** the sound on the radio.

indeed

Bill is happy **indeed** with his new bike.
Bill is **really** happy with his new bike.

inflammable

When something is **inflammable** it is **easy to set on fire.**
Gasoline is **inflammable.**
Matches are **inflammable.**

ink

Ink is a **coloured** liquid.
When we write with a pen we use **ink.**
All of the pictures in this book are made from different-coloured **inks.**

insect

An **insect** is a small **bug.**
A **bee** is an **insect.**
A **fly** is an **insect.**

inside

The horse is **inside** the stable.
The horse is **not outside** the stable.

instead

Mary ate cookies **instead** of the candy.
Mary ate cookies **in place** of the candy.

into

Please don't go **into** the cave alone.

invite

Did you **invite** Ann to your party?
Did you **ask** Ann **to come** to your party?

---

iron(1)

Iron is a hard, strong metal.
The lion's cage is made of **iron** bars.

---

iron(2)

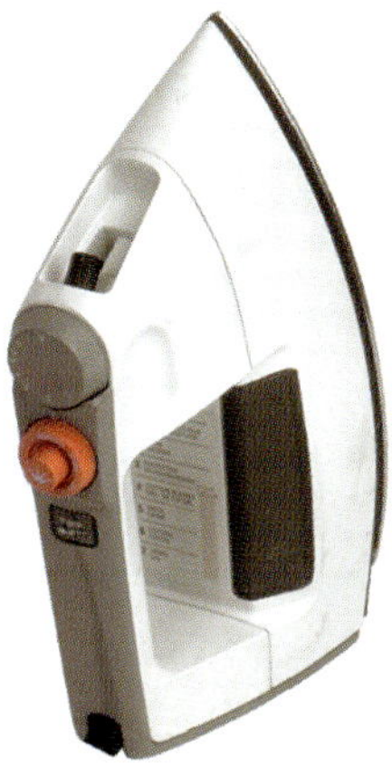

My mother uses an **iron** to press my clothes.

---

island

We had to go in a boat to reach the **island.**
The **island** is **a piece of land with water all around** it.

jacket

Tom wore his **jacket** to school.
Tom wore his **short coat** to school.

jail

When people do bad things they are put in **jail.** The **jail** is a building with bars on the windows and doors.

jam

Jam is good on bread.
Mother makes **jam** from different kinds of fruit.

joke

The teacher told the children a **joke.**
The teacher told the children a **funny story.**

jolly
jollier
jolliest

The man is very **jolly.**

journey

Father is going on a **journey.**

joy

Our visit brought **joy**
to Grandmother.
Our visit made
Grandmother **very happy.**

judge

Ann knows how to **judge** art.
Ann knows if the art is **good or bad.**

juice

Juice is the liquid part of a plant, fruit or vegetable.
I like orange **juice.** I also like tomato **juice.**

jump

The horse can **jump** over the fence.
The horse can **leap** over the fence.

just(1)

It is **just** one o'clock.
It is **exactly** one o'clock.

just(2)

Did you think the teacher's decision was **just?**
Did you think the teacher's decision was **fair and correct?**

kayak

A **kayak** is an Eskimo **canoe.**
This is a **kayak.**

keep
keeps
keeping
kept

I will **keep** Tom's dog for this week.
I will **take care of** Tom's dog this week.

kettle

Mother boils water
in a tea **kettle.**

key

We turn the **key** to lock our door.
We turn the **key** to unlock our door.

kick

Bill likes to **kick** the football.
Bill likes to **hit** the football **with** his **foot.**

kill

Jane saw the cat **kill** a bird.

kind(1)

Mother is **kind** to the baby.
Mother is **gentle and nice** to the baby.

kind(2)

What **kind** of ice cream do you want?
What **sort** of ice cream do you want?

king

Some countries have a **king** to lead the people.
Some countries have a **president** to lead the people.

kiss

Mary gave the baby a **kiss** on the cheek.
Mary **touched her lips to the baby's cheek.**

kitchen

I help my mother in the **kitchen.**
I help my mother in the **room where we cook food.**

kite

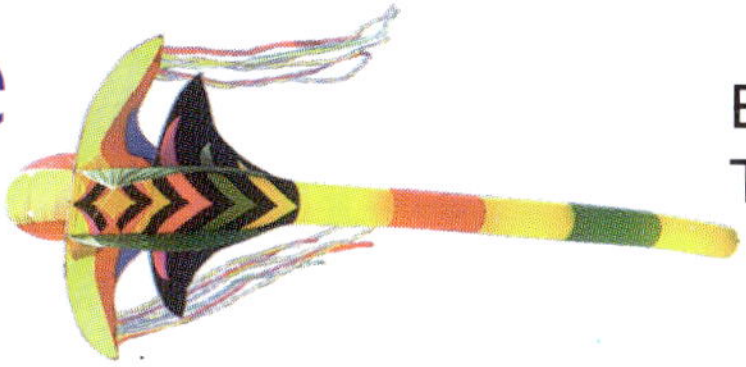

Bob likes to fly a **kite.**
The wind keeps the **kite** in the air.

kitten

Jane let me hold the **kitten.**
Jane let me hold the **baby cat.**

knee

Your **knee** is the joint in the middle of your leg.
Your leg bends at the **knee.**

knife
knives

We cut our food with a **knife.**
The **knife** has a handle and a sharp blade.
There are different kinds of **knives.**

knock

John **knocked** at the door.

know(1)
knows
knowing
knew
known

I **know** that Ann is at the door.
I **am sure** that Ann is at the door.

know(2)
knows
knowing
knew
known

Do you **know** Ann?
Have you met Ann?

laboratory
laboratories

A **laboratory** is a room or building where people work and discover new things.

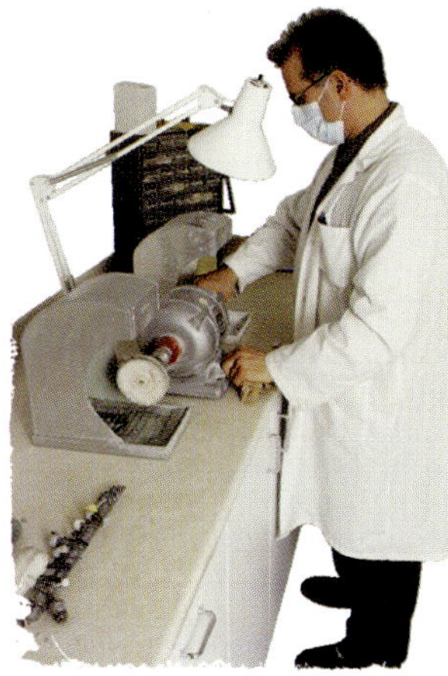

lace(1)

Can you **lace** your shoe?

lace(2)

The **lace** is a **string** that ties your shoe.

ladder

My father uses a **ladder** when he paints the house. The **ladder** is a set of steps that my father walks up to reach high places.

lady
ladies

The **lady** is a kind and polite **woman.** My mother is a **lady.**

lake

We ride a boat on the **lake.**

lamb

A baby sheep is a **lamb.**

lamp

I have a **lamp** near my bed.
I turn the **lamp** on when
I read.
The **lamp** gives light.

land(1)

The turtle can live on **land** but he likes the water.

land(2)

I like to watch the airplane **land.**
I like to watch the airplane **come down and touch the ground.**

lantern

The farmer carries a **lantern**
to the barn.

large
larger
largest

The elephant is a **large** animal.

last

Tom is **last** in line.
Tom is **at the end** of the line.
Jane took the **last** piece of candy.

late
later
latest

Bill was **late** for school.
Bill came **after the time** he should have been in school.

laugh

When we hear a funny story we **laugh.**
The children are watching the clown and they are **laughing.**

law

A **law** tells us what to do. We have **laws** in our country. We have **rules** in our country. We should obey the **law.**

lawn

The **lawn** is the ground around our house which is **covered with grass.** Father mows the **lawn.**

lay
lays
laying
laid

Did you **lay** your coat on the table?
Did you **put** your coat on the table?
Birds **lay** eggs.
Tom **laid** his coat on the table.
Tom **placed** his coat on the table.

lazy
lazier
laziest

A **lazy** person is a person that does not want to work.

lead(1)

Would you **lead** me to the lunchroom?
Would you **guide** me to the lunchroom?
I would like to **lead** the band.
I would like to **conduct** the band.

lead (2)

Lead is a heavy metal.

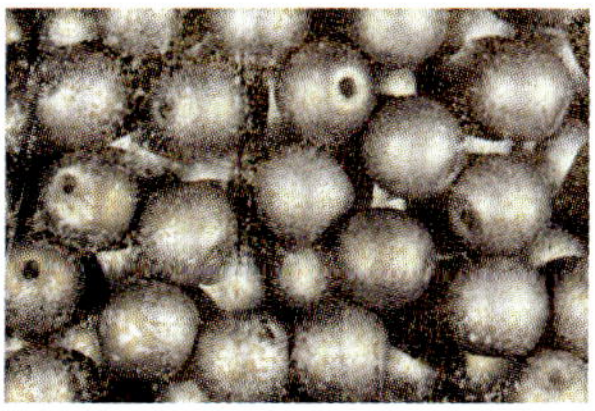

leaf
leaves

The wind blew a **leaf** from the tree.
There are many **leaves** on the tree.
Most plants have **leaves.** A page of this book is called a **leaf.**

---

lean(1)

The teacher said, "Please don't **lean** on the desk."
The teacher said, "Please don't **bend** over and **rest your elbows on the desk."**

---

lean(2)

This meat is very **lean.**
This meat has **no fat.**

---

leap
leaps
leaping
leapt

Bill can **leap** over the fence.
Bill can **jump** over the fence.

learn

I must **learn** to read well.
I must **find out how** to read well.

leave
leaves
leaving
left

What time will the train **leave** the station?

lecture

The teacher gave a **lecture** to the class about health.

left

Most people write with the right hand but some people write with their **left** hand.
Our **left** hand is on the **left** side of our body.

lemon

A **lemon** is a fruit.
The **lemon** is yellow and tastes sour.
We make **lemon**ade from **lemon** juice, water and sugar.

less
little
less
least

Jane has **less** money than Betty.
Jane **does not have as much** money as Betty.

letter(1)

I wrote a **letter** to my grandmother.
I put the **letter** in an envelope and mailed it to my grandmother.

letter(2)

A is a **letter** of the alphabet.
B is a **letter** of the alphabet.

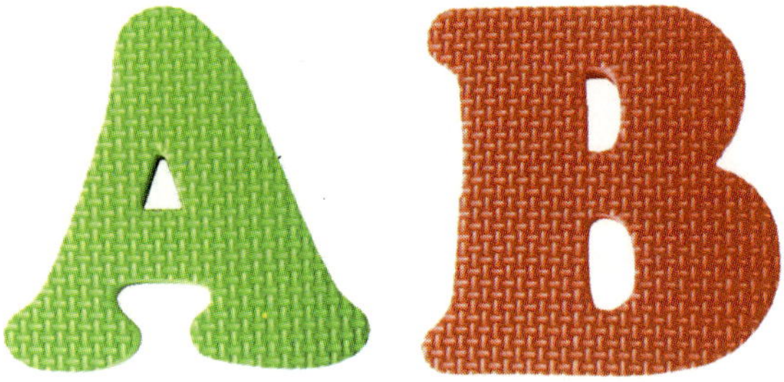

library
libraries

The **library** is a place where books are kept.
We go to the **library** to get books.
After we read the books we return them to the **library.**

lick

When the dog eats his food he will **lick** the dish.
The dog **uses his tongue to get all of the food out of** the dish.

lid

The box has a **lid** on it.
The box has a **cover** on it.

lie(1)
lies
lying
lied

Please don't **lie.**
Please don't **tell something that is not true.**

lie(2)
lay
lain

Francis likes to **lie** on the grass.

life
lives

Anything that lives has **life.**
A plant has **life.**

lift

Can you **lift** the box?
Can you **pick up** the box?

light(1)

At night we **turn on** the lamp.
The lamp makes **light** so that we can see.

light(2)

This box is **light.**
This box is **not heavy.**

light(3)

Jane's hair is of **light** colour.
Jane's hair is **not** of **dark** colour.

lightning

Sometimes when there is a storm we see **lightning** in the sky.
The **lightning** is caused by **electricity** in the sky.

like

Did you **like** the movie?
Did you **enjoy** the movie?
I **like** my new dress.
I **am happy with** my new dress.

limb

The bird built a nest on the **limb** of the tree.

line

The teacher said, "Please get in **line.**"
The teacher said, "Please get in a **row.**"
A telephone **line** is connected to the telephone.
A telephone **wire** is connected to the telephone.
Do you see the red **lines** on this page?

lion

The **lion** is a wild animal.
The **lion** eats meat.
I saw a **lion** in the zoo.

lip(1)

We have an upper **lip** and a lower **lip.**
The **lips** are part of our mouth.

lip(2)

A glass has a **lip.**

list

I wrote a **list** of names on the paper.

listen

You should **listen** to what the teacher is saying.
You should **pay attention** to what the teacher is saying.
Mary likes to **listen** to good music.

little
littler
littlest

Tom has a **little** brother.

live

I feed the kitten so that it will **live.**
Where do you **live?**
I **live** in a house.
When we go for camping we **live** in a tent.

load(1)

The truck brought a **load** of sand.
The truck brought a **pile** of sand.

load(2)

I watched the men **load** the truck.
I watched the men **fill** the truck.

location

My school is in this **location.**
My school is at this **place.**
My house is in another **location.**
My house is at another **place.**

lock

We **lock** the door at night.

log

Bill put a **log** on the fire.
The **log** will burn
and make
the room warm.
The **log** is a piece
of a tree.
A **log** cabin is
a small house
made with **logs.**

look(1)

Caroline will **look** for the book.

look(2)

The flowers **look** beautiful.

look(3)

The dogs **look** at each other.

loose
looser
loosest

The chain on Bill's bike is **loose.**
The chain on Bill's bike is **not tight.**
The dog is **loose.**
The dog is **free** and **not tied up.**

lose
loses
losing
lost

Jane does not want to **lose** her cat.
John **lost** the race.
John **did not win** the race.

loud

The bell makes a **loud** sound.

low

The bird is flying **low.** The bird is flying **near the ground.**
Father has a **low** voice. Mother has a high voice.

lullaby
lullabies

A **lullaby** is a **soft and tender song.**
Mother sings a **lullaby** to make the baby sleep.
The **lullaby** will lull the baby to sleep.

lunch
lunches

In the middle of the day we have **lunch.**
Lunch is the **meal** that we have **at noontime.**

mad
madder
maddest

The man in the movie was **mad.**
The man in the movie was **crazy.**

magic

The man on TV pulled rabbits out of his hat.
That was **magic.** It was a **trick** that I did not understand.

magnify

To **magnify** something is to make it appear larger.
My father's glasses will **magnify** the letters in the book.
My father's glasses will make the letters **look larger** and easier to read.
People use a telescope to **magnify** the stars.

mail

The postman brings us **mail.**
The postman brings us **letters.**

main

The **main** thing is to stay healthy.
The **most important** thing is to stay healthy.
When does the **main** show start?
When does the **most important** show start?

make
makes
making
made

Tom can **make** a birdhouse.
Tom can **build** a birdhouse.
The children sell lemonade to **make** money.
The children sell lemonade to **earn** money.

man
men

When a boy grows up, he becomes a **man.**
My brother is a boy. My father is a **man.**

manners

Jane has nice **manners.**
Jane has a nice **way of saying and doing things.**

many

There are **many** fishes in the pond.
There is a **large number** of fishes in the pond.

map

My father uses a **map** when we take a trip.
The **map** shows where the roads are.
The **map** shows which city and state we are in.

March

March is the third month of the year.

march

The children **march** in the parade.
The children **walk in step** with each other.

mark(1)

Mary got a good **mark** in her test.
Mary got a good **grade** in her test.

mark(2)

Please don't **mark** the wall.
Please don't **write** on the wall.

market

We go to the **market** to buy things.

marry

When a man and a woman **marry,** they become husband and wife.
When I grow up,
I will **marry** someone.

match (1)

Helen jumped five feet.
Can you **match** that?
Helen jumped five feet.
Can you **do the same?**

match(2)
matches

If you strike a **match** it will make a flame.
You should not play with **matches.**

master

Jim is the dog's **master.**
Jim is the dog's **owner.**

meal

Breakfast is the morning **meal.** Lunch is a **meal** taken in the afternoon.

mean (1)
means
meaning
meant

What does this word **mean?**

mean (2)
means
meaning
meant

What do you **mean?**

mean (3)

The boy is **mean.**
The boy is **not kind and pleasant.**

measure

We **measure** things to find out their size or weight or amount.

meat

Meat is food that we get from animals.
A **steak** is **meat.**
A **pork chop** is **meat.**

meet
meets
meeting
met

Ann and Mary will **meet** after school.
Ann and Mary will **get together.**

melon

A **melon** is good to eat.

melt

When the sun shines, the ice will **melt.**
When the sun shines, the ice will **turn back to water.**

memorize

Did you **memorize** the song?
Did you **learn** the song **by heart?**
Can you sing the song without looking at the song book?

merry

The boys and girls are **merry.**
The boys and girls are **joyful and happy.**

middle

There are two holes in the **middle** of the button.
There are two holes in the **centre** of the button.

milk

We drink **milk** to stay healthy.
Milk comes from cows.
I watched the farmer **milk** the cow.
The baby is drinking **milk.**

mind

Sue will **mind** the baby.

mine(1)

This book is **mine.**
This book **belongs to me.**

mine(2)

A **mine** is a large hole in the ground.
Men dig coal out of a **mine.**
Men dig gold ore out of a **mine.**

mistake

Jane made a **mistake** in her test.
Jane made an **error.**
Jane answered the question **wrong**.

mix

I watched my mother **mix** the cake.
Oil and water do not **mix.**
Oil and water do not **blend together.**

money

We buy things with **money.**

monkey

A **monkey** is an **animal** that lives in the jungle.
We see **monkeys** in the zoo.
This is a **monkey.**

monstrous

The giant in the story was **monstrous.**
The giant in the story was **very large and ugly.**
The giant looked like a monster.

moon

The **moon** shines at night.
The **moon** moves around our earth every 29and 1/2 days.

more
most

Betty drank her milk but she wanted **more.**
She wanted **another** glass of milk.
Ann has **more** pencils than Jane.
Ann has a **greater number** of pencils.

mother

My **mother** is married to my father.
My **mother** takes care of me. I love my **mother.**

mountain

The **mountain** is a piece of land that is much higher than the land around it.
The **mountain** is larger than a hill.

mouth

We eat and speak with our **mouth.**
The dog caught the ball with his **mouth.**

move

Please **move** your coat.
Please **put** your coat **in a different place.**
The truck will **move** soon.
The truck will **go to a different place** soon.

music

We love to hear **music.**
The **beautiful sound the band makes** is **music.**
We sing in **music** class.

must

You **must** go to school today.
You **have to** go to school today.

myself

I must take care of **myself.**
I don't go into the woods by **myself.**
I don't go into the woods **alone.**

name

What is your **name?** What are you **called?**
The cat's **name** is **Tom.** We call the cat **Tom.**
The bird in the tree is a crow. **Crow** is the bird's **name.**

nap

The dog is taking a **nap.**

napkin

A **napkin** is a piece of cloth or paper. A **napkin** protects our clothes when we eat. We wipe our fingers and lips with a **napkin.**

narrate

The teacher asked Sally to **narrate** a story to the class.
The teacher asked Sally to **tell** a story to the class.

narrow

The bridge we crossed was **narrow.**
The bridge we crossed was **not wide.**

near

The school is **near** Jane's house. The school is **close** to Jane's house.
The school is **not far from** Jane's house.

N

neat

You should keep your room **neat.**
You should keep your room **clean and in order.**

neck

Father wears a tie around his **neck.**
The dog has a collar around his **neck.**
The **neck** is **between the head and shoulders.**

need

I **need** a pencil to write a letter. I **must have** a pencil to write a letter. When it rains, we **need** a raincoat.
When it rains, we **should have** a raincoat.

neighbour

John is Jack's **neighbour.** John **lives next door** to Jack.

nest

The birds built a **nest** in the tree.
The bird lays eggs in the **nest.** Soon the eggs will hatch and baby birds will live in the **nest.**

net

John caught a fish with the **net.** The **net** is made of string. Water runs through the **net** but the fish cannot get out.

never

Jane can **never** run as fast as Jim.

new

Tom's coat is **new.**
Tom's coat is **not old.**
Mother has a **new** hair style.
Mother has a **modern** hair style.

next

The baby sleeps **next** to the teddy bear.
The baby sleeps **beside** the teddy bear.
The boy **next** to Tom is Sam.
The boy **nearest** to Tom is Sam.

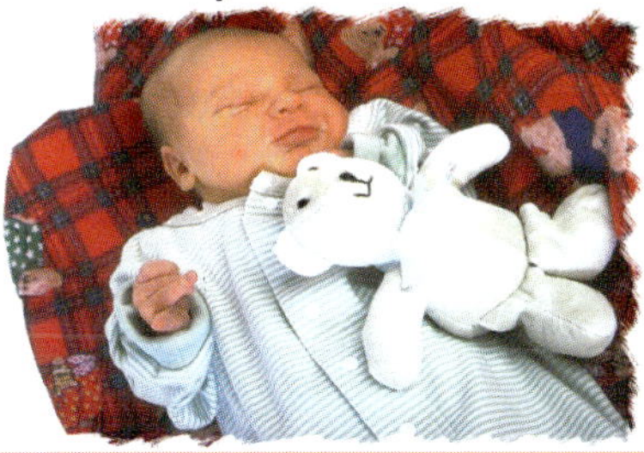

nice
nicer
nicest

Mary is very **nice.**

nine

We have **nine** players on our baseball team.
When we count **nine** we say:
1, 2, 3, 4, 5, 6, 7, 8, **9.**

N

nod

When the baby is sleepy her head will **nod.**
When the baby is sleepy her head will **bow.**
Her head will **move up and down.**

noise

A **noise** will wake the baby.
A **loud sound** will wake the baby.

none

The children looked for seashells.
There was **none.**
There was **no one** in the class.

noon

Noon is 12 o'clock in the daytime.

North

The birds are flying toward **North.**
The birds are flying toward the **top part of our earth.**
The top part of a map is **North.**

note

Jane wrote Mary a **note.** Jane wrote Mary a **short letter.**
Bill made a **note** of which books he would like.
Bill **wrote down** which books he would like.

nothing

There is **nothing** left on my plate.
There is **not a thing** left on my plate.

notice

Did you **notice** Mary's new dress?
Did you **see** Mary's new dress?

nourish

To **nourish** is to **feed.**
We must **nourish** our body to stay healthy and grow.
We must **feed** our body to stay healthy and grow.

now

The sun is shining **now.**
The sun is shining **at this time.**

number

A **number** tells us **how many** there are of something. I am **six** years old. Six is the **number** of years I have lived. Each **number** has a name. When we count from 1 to 10 we say: one, two, three, four, five, six, seven, eight, nine, ten.

nurse

A **nurse** takes care of sick people.
A **nurse** also takes care of children and older people.

nut

A **nut** is the seed of a tree or plant. A **nut** has a shell. Some **nuts** are good to eat. Walnuts, pecans and acorns are **nuts.**

oak

Oak is the name of one kind of tree.
Acorns grow on **oak** trees.

oats

The farmer grows **oats** in a field.
The grains from **oats** are used to make different kinds of food.

obey

John taught the dog to **obey** him.
The dog **does what he is told to do.**

object (1)

Anything that you can see or touch is an **object.**
A pencil is an **object.**
A piece of paper is an **object.**

object (2)

Would you **object** if the dog came with us?

oblong

When something is longer than it is wide we say it is **oblong.**
The shape of a loaf of bread is **oblong.**
The loaf of bread is **long and less wide.**

ocean

The **ocean** is **the large body of salty water that covers more than two-thirds of our earth.**
The **ocean** is divided into five great oceans.
The names are Pacific, Atlantic, Indian, Arctic and Antarctic.

odd (1)

I have one **odd** sock.
I have **one** sock **left over.**

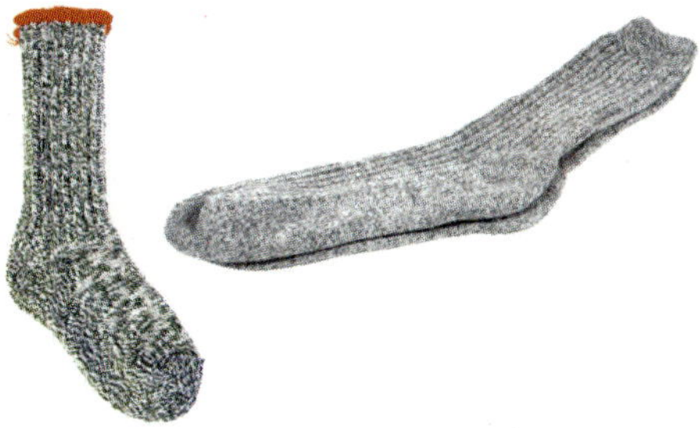

odd (2)

I believe the story, but it sounds **odd.**
I believe the story, but it sounds **strange.**

off

The car is **off** the road.
The car is **not on** the road.

office

An **office** is **a room where people work.**
Dad has a desk in his **office.**

often

Jane **often** plays the piano.
Jane plays the piano **many times.**

old

The man is **old.** The man is **not young.**
My bike is **old.** My bike is **not new.**

once

Mary was late for school only **once.**

one

There is **one** apple left.
There is a **single** apple left.
There were two apples but Bill ate **one.**
One should brush one's teeth every day.
A person should brush his teeth every day.

only (1)

Mary has **only** one pencil.
Mary has **just** one pencil.

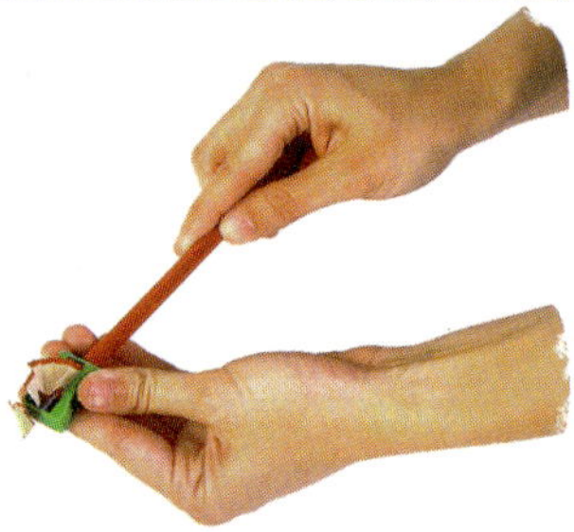

only(2)

This is the **only** school in town.
There is **no other** school in town.

open

The window is **open.**
The window is **not closed.**
The door is **open.**

orangutang

The **orangutang** is a large ape. The **orangutang** lives in the jungle.

order

Do you have your room in **order?**
Do you have **everything in the right place?**
The captain gave the soldiers an **order.**
The captain **told** the soldiers **what they had to do.**

organ

The **organ** makes beautiful music.
We have an **organ** at church.
Different parts of our body are called **organs.** Our heart is an **organ.**
Our liver is an **organ.**

other

Are there **other** children coming to your party?
Are there **more** children coming to your party?
The **other** children will be late. **All the rest** of the children will be late.
I will ride the **other** bus for home. I will ride a **different** bus for home.

O

our

This is **our** house.
It **belongs to us.**

out (1)

Jane took her gift **out** of the box.
Jane **took it from inside** the box.
My parents went **out** tonight.
My parents went **away** from the house.

out (2)

The light is **out.**
The light is **not turned on.**

oven

We baked a cake in the **oven.**
The **oven** is inside
the stove.

over (1)

When will the play be **over?**
When will the play be **finished?**

over (2)

John jumped **over** the fence.
John jumped **across** the fence.
Mary is holding an umbrella **over** her head.
Mary is holding an umbrella **above** her head.

over (3)

I must do my homework **over.**
I must do my homework **again.**

over (4)

Jane jumped **over** twenty times.
Jane jumped **more than** twenty times.

owe

I **owe** Bill money.
I am in **debt** to Bill.

owl

The **owl** is a bird.
The **owl** has big eyes.
The **owl** sleeps during the day and looks for food at night.

own

I **own** two dogs and one cat.
I **have** two dogs and one cat.

pack

We **pack** our clothes when we take a trip.
We **put together** our clothes when we take a trip.

package

The postman brought Linda a **package.**
The postman brought
Linda a **box wrapped in paper.**

pad

I write on a **pad** of paper.

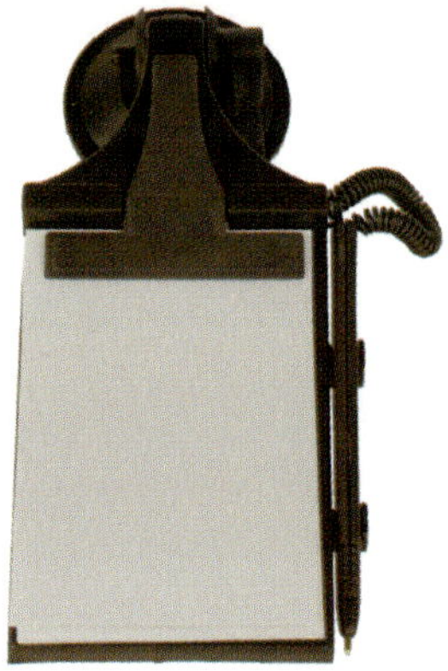

page

Each piece of paper in this book is a **page.**
Each **page** has a number in the lower corner.
Which **page** are you reading?

pail

Mary filled the **pail** with water.
Mary filled the **bucket** with water.

pain

Tom has a **pain** in his head.
His head **hurts.** Tom has a **headache.**

paint

Jack will **paint** his house green.
Jack will **colour** his house with green **paint.**
I like to **paint** pictures. I use many colours of **paint.**

pair

A **pair** means **two of a kind.**
Jane has a **pair** of skates. I am wearing a **pair** of shoes.

palace

A **palace** is a **large and beautiful house.**
The king and the queen lived in a **palace.**

pale
paler
palest

Your face is **pale.** Are you sick?
Your face is **almost white.** Are you sick?

palm

Palm trees grow in places where the weather is warm.
The inside of your hand is called the **palm.**

pan

Mother fries eggs in a **pan.**
This is a **pan.**

pansy
pansies

A **pansy** is a small beautiful flower.
There are many different colours of **pansies.**

pant

The dog will **pant** when he is hot and tired.
The dog will **breathe hard and fast.**

paper

We write on **paper.**
This book is made of **paper.**
We wrap things with **paper.**

parachute

The man used a **parachute** when he jumped from an airplane.
The **parachute** was fastened to his body.
The **parachute** opened and the man floated slowly to the ground.

parade

Did you see the circus **parade?**
The band played music and people in bright costumes **marched** in the street.
There were soldiers in the **parade.**

parcel

The postman brought a **parcel.**

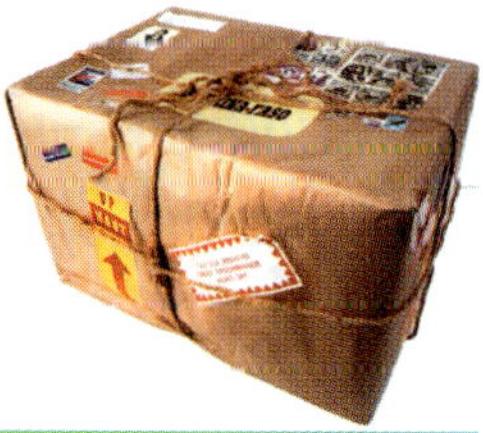

parent

I love my **parents.**

park(1)

The children had a picnic in the **park.**
The **park** has trees, green grass and a lake.

park(2)

My father will **park** the car in the garage.

part

Which **part** of the chicken do you like?
Which **piece** of the chicken do you like?
Jane took a **part** in the show.
Jane took a **role** in the show.

party
parties

I invited ten children to my birthday **party.**
The boys and girls ate ice cream and played games. People **get together** at a **party** to **have fun.**

pass

The little car will **pass** the big car.
It is raining but it will soon **pass.**

past

There were no airplanes in the **past.**

pat

Mary wants to give the horse a **pat.**

path

We walked on a **path** through the woods.
The **path** is a small dirt road.

pattern

Mother gave me a **pattern** to make a doll dress.
Mother gave me a **design** to make a doll dress.

paw

The dog digs a hole with his **paw.**
The **paw** is the dog's **foot** and it has claws on it.

pay
pays
paying
paid

Did you **pay** for the book?

Did you **give money in exchange** for the book?

pelican

The **pelican** is a large water bird.
The **pelican** has webbed feet for swimming.
The **pelican** has a pouch on its lower bill for scooping up fish.

pen

We write with a **pen**.

pencil

Sometimes I write with a pen and sometimes I write with a **pencil.**
A **pencil** makes marks with lead.

people

We have many **people** in our country.
We have many **persons** in our country.

period(1)

The dot at the end of this sentence is a **period.**

period(2)

There was a **period** when my father was out of work.
There was a **time** when my father was out of work.

person

Everyone is a **person.**
You are a **person.**

piano

Jane can play the **piano.**
The **piano** is a musical instrument.

pick

I like to **pick** cherries from the tree.
I like to **gather** cherries from the tree.

picnic

The girls and boys are having a **picnic.**
They are **eating food outdoors.**

picture (1)

Bill drew a **picture** of Mary.
Bill drew an **image** of Mary.

picture (2)

Do you like the **pictures** in this book?

pie

My mother made an apple **pie.**

piece

I ate a **piece** of the pie.
I ate a **part** of the pie.

pile

The apples are in a **pile.**
The apples are in a **heap.**
The apples are **bunched** together.

pilgrim

A **pilgrim** is a person that travels to a holy place.
The **pilgrim** wanders from one place to another.

pillow

The **pillow** is filled with feathers and is very soft.
The baby's head is on the **pillow.**

pilot

The man who flies the airplane is a **pilot.**
The man that guides a boat is a **pilot.**

pine

A **pine** tree is called an **evergreen tree.**
The **pine** tree stays green all year.
The fruits of a **pine** tree are cones.

pipe(1)

Liquids move through a **pipe**.
Liquids move through a **tube**.

pipe(2)

Sometimes my father smokes a **pipe.**

pitcher

My mother keeps cold water in the **pitcher.**

place(1)

The teacher asked, "Is everyone in his **place?"**
The teacher asked, "Is everyone in his **position?"**

place(2)

Please **place** the book on the shelf.
Please **put** the book on the shelf.

plain(1)

Betty is wearing a **plain** dress.
The dress has **no trimmings.**

point

The pencil has a **point**.
The pencil has a **sharp point.**

pole(1)

The flag is fastened to a **pole.**

pole(2)

We use a **pole** when we go fishing.
The **pole** is a **long stick** with a string and hook tied to the end.

policeman
policemen

A **policeman** protects people.
Most **policemen** wear uniforms and have a shiny badge.
Sometimes a **policeman** stands at the street corner to tell us when to cross the street.

polite
politer
politest

Joan is **polite.**
She has **good manners.**

pond

A pond is a **small lake.**
Jack and Tom go fishing in the **pond.**

pony
ponies

Did you ever ride a **pony?**

A **pony** is a **small horse.**

porch

Our **porch** is in the front of the house.
The **porch** has a roof and a floor.
Our **porch** does not have walls.

possible

I will get to school on time if **possible**.

postman
postmen

The **postman** brings letters to our house.

pot

The **pot** is a big bowl for cooking.
Mother cooks food in a **pot.**

poultry

The chickens on a farm are called **poultry.**
The ducks and geese are also **poultry.**

pound

Please don't **pound** on the door.
Please don't **bang** on the door.

pour

Watch the water **pour** from the pipe.

practice

Practice makes a man perfect.
Jane will **play her piano lesson several times.**

praise

The teacher will **praise** Bill's work if he tries hard. The teacher will **speak well** of Bill's work if he tries hard.

precious

My mother's ring is **precious.**

prepare

You must **prepare** for the reading test. You must **study** for the reading test. Did you **prepare** the picnic lunch? Did you **make** the picnic lunch?

present

The children played a game but Bill was not **present.**
The children played a game but Bill was not **there.**
We gave Mary a birthday **present.**
We gave Mary a birthday **gift.**

pretend

Jill will **pretend** that she is a queen.
Jill will **make believe** that she is a queen.

pretty
prettier
prettiest

Do you think the girl is **pretty?**
Do you think the girl is
nice to look at?

price

The **price** of the pencil is five rupees.
The **cost** of the pencil is five rupees.

primer

I learnt to read from a **primer.**
I learnt to read from a **beginner's book.**

prince

The young boy is a **prince.**
The prince is the **son of a king and queen.**

princess

The girl is a **princess.**
She is the **daughter of a king and queen.**

principal

Mr. Brown is the **principal** of our school.
Mr. Brown is the **head teacher** of our school.

prize

Bob won a **prize** for winning the race.
Bob won an **award** for winning the race.
Bob won the **prize** for running faster than anyone else.

promise

Do you **promise** to be good?
Do you **say** you will be good?
When you make a **promise, you do what you say.**

promote

The teacher will **promote** you if you study hard.
The teacher will **put you in a higher grade** if you study hard.

prompt

Jane is always **prompt.**
Jane is always **on time.**

proper

Is this the **proper** coat to wear to the party?
Is this the **right** coat to wear to the party?

protect

The policeman will **protect** us.
The policeman will **see that nothing harms** us.

proud

Bill drew a picture and he is **proud** of it.
Bill drew a picture and he is **pleased** with it.

pudding

Do you like the **pudding?**
Do you like the **soft, sweet dessert?**
Mother made chocolate **pudding.**

pull

John will **pull** the wagon when the baby wants to ride.
John will **move** the wagon toward him.
I like to **pull** apples from the tree. I will **gather** apples from the tree.

pumpkin

A **pumpkin** is a large, orange-coloured fruit.
The **pumpkin** grows on a vine.
We can cut a face in the **pumpkin.**
Pumpkin pie is good to eat.

punctual

Jane is always **punctual.**
Jane is always **on time.**

pupil

Tom is a **pupil** in this school.
Tom is **one of the children** in this school.

puppy
puppies

A baby dog is called a **puppy.** Bob has two **puppies.**

pure
purer
purest

The water from the spring is **pure.**
The water from the spring is **clear and clean.**

purse

Mother keeps her money in a **purse.**
A **purse** is a **small bag** used for carrying things.

pursue

We watched the dog **pursuing** the cat.
We watched the dog **tracking** the cat.

push

The big boy should not **push** the smaller boy.

put
puts
putting
put

John **put** the book on the table.
John **placed** the book on the table.

Q

quarrel

You should not **quarrel** with your brother.
You should not **say angry words to each other.**

quarter

When we divide something into four equal parts we call each piece one **quarter.**

queen

Some countries have a **queen.**
Some countries have a **woman that rules the people.**

quench

The water will **quench** the fire. The water will **put out** the fire.

question

When you say, **"Where is the dog?",** you have asked a **question.**

Q

quick

Let's take a **quick** walk. Let's take a **fast** walk.

quiet

Please be **quiet** or you will wake the baby. Please **do not make noise** or you will wake the baby.
The sea is very **quiet.** The sea is very **calm.**

quit
quits
quitting

Tom **quit** working because he was tired.
Tom **stopped** working because he was tired.

quite

This cake is **quite** good.
This cake is **really** good.

quiz
quizzes

We had a spelling **quiz** at school.
We had a **test to see** how well we could spell.

rabbit

A **rabbit** is an **animal.** The **rabbit** has long ears and a short tail.

race

Bob and Tom ran a **race.**
They ran a **race** to find out which boy is fastest.

raccoon

The **raccoon** is a small animal that lives in the woods.
The **raccoon** sleeps during the day and looks for food at night.
A **raccoon** likes to climb trees.

radio

We turn on the **radio** to hear music.

rail(1)

This is a **rail** fence.

rail(2)

The train runs on **rails.**

rain

We expect some **rain** today.
We expect some **drops of water will fall.**
It **rained** yesterday. It was **raining** last night.

raincoat

Jane will wear her **raincoat** today.
The **raincoat** will keep Jane dry.

raise(1)

Raise your hand if you know the answer.
Lift up your hand if you know the answer.

raise(2)

The farmer **raises** chickens.

rake

A **rake** is a tool.
We **rake** leaves with a **rake.**

rat

A **rat** is an **animal.**
A cat is larger than a **rat.**

raven

The **raven** is a large, black bird that looks like a crow.
The **raven** has a sharp beak.

reach

Jane cannot **reach** the book on the top shelf.
Jane cannot **stretch out her arm and touch** the book.

read
reads
reading

Bill can **read** very well.
Bill can **look at the words and understand what they mean.**
The man is **reading** to my father.

ready

Our dinner is **ready.**
Our dinner has been **cooked and is on the table.**
We are **ready** to eat dinner.

real

The story that Mary told was **real.**
The story that Mary told was **true.**

reason

Bill told the teacher the **reason** for his being late.
Bill told the teacher **why** he was late.

receive

Jane will **receive** many gifts on her birthday.
Jane will **get** many gifts on her birthday.

recognize

Do you **recognize** the boy walking with Tom?
Did you **know** the boy before now?
Do you **remember** his name?

red
redder
reddest

Fire engines are usually **red.**

remain

Please **remain** in your seat.
Please **stay** in your seat.
Bob ate one apple and
one **remained.**

remember

Do you **remember** the date of your birthday?
Do you **have in mind** the date of your birthday?
You should **not forget** the date of your birthday.

remove

Betty will **remove** her wet coat.

rent

We **rent** our house.
Another person owns the house but we **pay for using** the house.

repeat

Would you **repeat** the answer?
Would you **say** it **again?**
To **repeat is to do something more than one time.**

reply

What was your **reply** to the question?
What was your **answer** to the question?

report

Jack gave a **report** of his vacation.
Jack **told all about** his vacation.

resident

My father is a **resident** of our town.
My father is **a person who lives in** our town.

rest

Tom finished his work and now he will **rest.**
Tom finished his work and now he will **sit still for a while.**

return

You may read my book but you must **return** it.

rhinoceros

The **rhinoceros** is a large, thick-skinned animal that lives in Africa and Asia. A **rhinoceros** eats plants. A **rhinoceros** has a horn on his nose.

ribbon

Jane has a blue **ribbon** in her hair.
Jane has a blue **strip of cloth** in her hair.
We tie a gift with **ribbon.**

rich

Some people are **rich** and some people are poor.
Some people **have much money** and some people have none.

riddle

A **riddle** is a question that is hard to answer.
In fact, it is a **puzzle**.

ride
rides
riding
rode
ridden

Jack likes to **ride** the pony.
Jack likes to be **carried** by the pony.
Yesterday, he **rode** the pony for one hour.

right(1)

Betty writes with her **right** hand.
She holds the paper with
her left hand.

right(2)

Bob gave the **right** answer.
Bob gave the **correct** answer.

ring(1)

The teacher said, "Please get in a **ring.**"
The teacher said, "Please get in a **circle.**"

ring(2)

My mother has a gold **ring.**
A **ring** is a **circle** of gold.

ring(3)
rings
ringing
rang
rung

Did you hear the telephone **ring?**
Did you hear the telephone **jingle?**

rip

The dog **ripped** the doll.
The dog **tore** the doll.

ripe
riper
ripest

The melon is **ripe.**
The melon is **not raw.**
The melon is **ripe** so it is good to eat.

rise
rises
rising
rose
risen

We watched the sun **rise.**
We watched the sun **come up.**
The sun **rose** over the mountain.
The sun has **risen.**

river

The Amazon is a **river.**

road

A **road** is a way made for going between places by car.
Sometimes we call the **road** a **highway.**

roar

Have you heard a lion **roar?**
Have you heard a lion **make a loud noise?**
A dog barks but a lion **roars.**

roast

Mother will put the meat in the oven to **roast.**
Mother will put the meat in the oven to **cook.**

robin

Robin is the name of a bird.
A **robin** has a red breast.

rock(1)

Bill threw a **rock** in the water.
Bill threw a **large stone** in the water.

rough(1)

The sea was **rough**. It was **stormy**.

rough(2)

The board is **rough**. The board is **not smooth**.

rough(3)

The road is **rough**. It is **bumpy**.

round

A baseball is **round**. A circle is **round**.
When something is shaped like a circle it is **round**.

route

My father must decide which **route** to take to the mountains.
My father must decide which **road** to take to the mountains.

row(1)

Mother planted the flowers in a **row**.
Mother planted the flowers in a **line**.

row(2)

We **row** to make the boat move. We use oars to **row a boat**.

rub

I **rub** my hands together to get them warm. When something hurts I **rub** it with my hand.

rubber

Rubber is made from the sap of a **rubber** tree.
A **rubber** ball will bounce.
The tyres on a car are made of **rubber**.

rude

Bill was **rude** to the other boy. Bill was **not nice** to the other boy. Bill used **poor manners**.

rug

The **rug** is a cover for the floor. The **rug** is soft to walk on. I have a small **rug** beside my bed.

rule(1)

The king's job is to **rule** his country.
The king's job is to **lead** his country.

rule(2)

In school we have **rules** to go by.
In school we have **laws** to go by.

run
runs
running
ran
run

Bob can **run** faster than Bill.
Bob can **move his feet faster** than Bill.

rush

Jane is late and she must **rush**.
She is late and she must **walk quickly**.

sack

My mother bought
a **sack** of potatoes.
My mother bought
a **bag** of potatoes.

sad
sadder
saddest

Mary lost her kitten and she is **sad.**
Mary lost her kitten and she
is **unhappy.**

safe
safer
safest

I feel **safe** when the policeman helps me cross the street.
I feel **free from danger** when the policeman helps me cross the street.

sail

The sailboat has **sails** on it.
Wind blows against the **sails** and makes the boat go.

sailor

A **sailor** is a man that works on a boat.
The **sailor** sails on big boats.

salad

Mother made a vegetable **salad.**
She mixed different kinds of vegetables and put **salad** dressing on them.
Sometimes we have fruit **salad.**

sale

Tom has a new bike and his old bike is for **sale.**
Tom wants to sell his old bike.

salt

Most **salt** comes from out of the ground.
We put **salt** on food to make the food taste better.
The ocean has **salt** in it.

same(1)

Mary's dress and my dress are the **same.**

same(2)

We buy our clothes at the **same** store.

sand

The children play in the **sand** at the seashore.
Sand is tiny pieces of rock.
The desert is covered with **sand.**

sandwich sandwiches

When we put food between two pieces of bread we make a **sandwich.**

satisfy

We gave the baby a bottle of milk to **satisfy** her.
We gave the baby a bottle of milk to **please** her.

save(1)

I **save** my money in a coin bank.
I **keep** my money in a coin bank.

save(2)

Tom tried to **save** the bird's life.
Tom tried to **protect** the bird's life.

saw

A **saw** is a tool. A **saw** cuts wood.
Father will **saw** the tree down.
Father will **cut** the tree down.

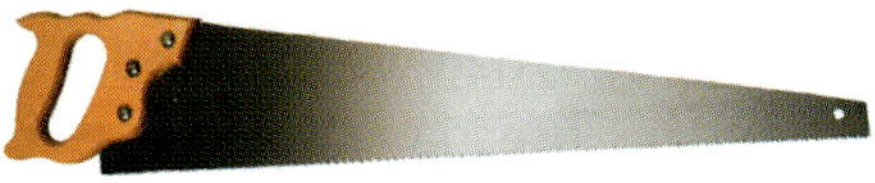

say
says
saying
said

When you **speak** you **say** something.
Did you want to **say** something to me?
Did you want to **tell** me something?

scale(1)

Bill stands on the **scale** to weigh himself.
Bill stands on the **weighing machine** to weigh himself.

scale(2)

Almost all fishes are covered with **scales.**

scare

The dog barked at Jane but it did not **scare** her.
The dog barked at Jane but she was not **frightened.**

scarf
scarves

My father wears a **scarf** around his neck.
He wears a **piece of cloth** around his neck to keep him warm.

scatter

We watched the farmer **scatter** the grass seed.
We watched the farmer **throw the seed here and there.**
He **threw** the seeds **in all directions.**

scene(1)

Is this the **scene** where the accident happened?
Is this the **place** where the accident happened?

scene(2)

A **scene** is a part of a play.

schedule

Father has a train **schedule**. The **schedule** is a **list of the times** the trains leave and arrive at the train station. When we go on vacation we make a **schedule.** We make a **list of the things we plan to do.**

school

We go to **school** to learn.
We have teachers in our **school.**
We have pupils in our **school.**

schoolroom

A **schoolroom** is a room in the schoolhouse.
Our **schoolroom** has a blackboard and bookcases.

scissors

Scissors are used to cut paper and cloth. The barber cuts my hair with **scissors.**

scold

If you are bad, the teacher will **scold** you. If you are bad, the teacher will be **angry and find fault with you.** She will **say sharp words** to you.

scooter

John rides on his **scooter.** He puts one foot on the **scooter** and pushes with the other foot to make it go.

scrap

Tom gave the dog a **scrap** of meat. Tom gave the dog a **small piece** of meat. A **scrap** of paper is a **small piece** of paper.

scrape

Ann spilled paint on her desk. She will **scrape** the paint off.

scratch(1)

Bill has a **scratch** on his hand.
Bill has a **little cut** on his hand.

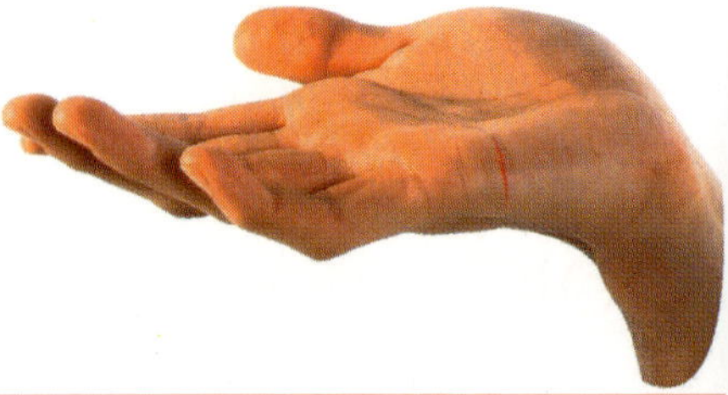

scratch(2)

When I have an itch I **scratch** it with my fingers.

scream

Did you hear the baby **scream?**
Did you hear the baby give a **loud cry?**

screen

When we watch television, we look at the television **screen.**

scrub

Jane helped her mother **scrub** the floor.
Jane helped her mother **wash** the floor.

sea

The **sea** is a large body of salty water.
An ocean is called the **sea.**
Whales swim in the **sea.**

seal

The **seal** is an animal that lives in the ocean.
The **seal** lives where the water is cold.
The **seal** eats fish.

season

Winter is a **season** of the year.
Winter is a **time** of the year.
The four **seasons** in a year are winter, spring, summer and autumn.

seat

The teacher said, "Please go to your **seat."**
The teacher said, "Please go to your **chair** and **sit down."**

second

Tom finished the race first.
Bill finished the race **second**.
A **second** is a **short period of time.**
There are sixty **seconds** in a minute.

see

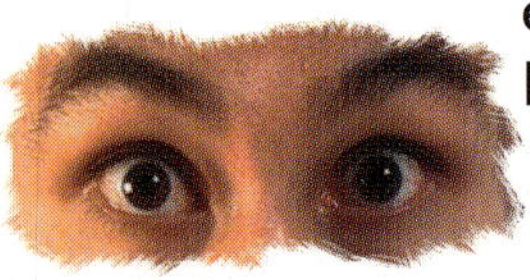

We **see** with our eyes. We **look at things** with our eyes. If you get sick, you must **see** the doctor.
If you get sick, you must **visit** the doctor.

seed

A plant grows from a **seed.**
My mother plants **seeds** in the flower garden.
A farmer plants **seeds** to raise food.
An acorn is a **seed.** An oak tree grows from an **acorn.**

seem

Bob does not **seem** angry. Bob does not **look** angry. Does the weather **seem** hot to you?
Does the weather **appear** hot to you?

seesaw

The children are playing on the **seesaw.**
It goes up and down.

seize

Did you see the cat **seize** the mouse?
Did you see the cat **take hold of** the mouse?

seldom

I **seldom** go to the zoo.
I **rarely** go to the zoo.
I **do not often** go to the zoo.

select

Please **select** the book that you want.
Please **pick out** the book that you want.

sell

Joe is trying to **sell** his newspapers.
Joe is trying to **get money for** his newspapers.

semicircle

Can you draw a **semicircle?** A **semicircle** is a half circle.
This is a circle. This is a **semicircle.**

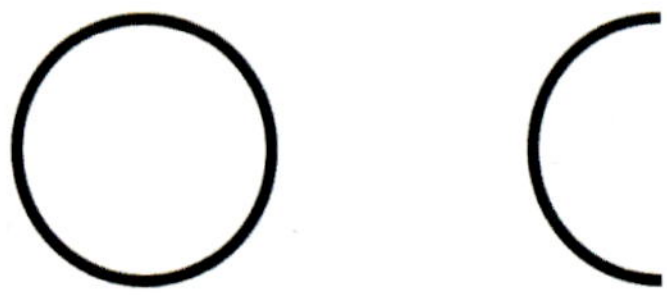

send
sends
sending
sent

I will **send** grandmother a gift on her birthday.
My mother will **send** me to bed at nine o'clock.
My mother will **make me go** to bed at nine o'clock.

sense

There is no **sense** in going out tonight. There is no **reason** for going out tonight. My mother has good **sense.** My mother **knows the right thing to do.**

sentence

A **sentence** is words put together to tell or ask something.
The line of words that you are reading is a **sentence**

separate

Bob will **separate** the bad apples from the good apples.
Bob will **take** the bad apples **away from** the good apples.

serve

Mother will **serve** our food. Mother will **wait upon** us.
Mother will **bring our food to** us.

set(1)
sets
setting

Please **set** the chair in the corner.

Please **put** the chair in the corner.

set(2)

We have a new **set** of dishes.
We have a new **group** of dishes.

seven

Seven is a number.
When you count **seven** you say: 1, 2, 3, 4, 5, 6, **7.**
I was **seven** years old last year.

sew
sews
sewing
sewed
sewn

Do you know how to **sew?**
Do you know how to **connect cloth together with a needle and thread?**
Mother **sews** on a **sewing** machine.

shade(1)

We have a **shade** over the window.
The **shade** keeps the light out of the room.

---

shade(2)

When the sun is too hot, we sit in the **shade** of a tree.

---

shadow

The **shadow** of a tree is the shape made by the sun shining around the tree. Did you see your **shadow** on the ground?
You were standing between your **shadow** and the sun.

---

shake(1)
shakes
shaking
shook
shaken

The boys **shake** the tree to get the apples.
The boys **move** the tree **back and forth quickly.**

---

shake(2)
shakes
shaking
shook
shaken

I will **shake** hands with my new friend.

shape

The **shape** of a baseball is **round.** Sometimes the **shape** of a book is **square.**

share

Jane and Betty will **share** the picnic lunch.
Each girl will **have a part** of the picnic lunch.

sharp(1)

The knife is very **sharp.**
The point of the pencil is **sharp.**
The point of the pencil is **very fine.**

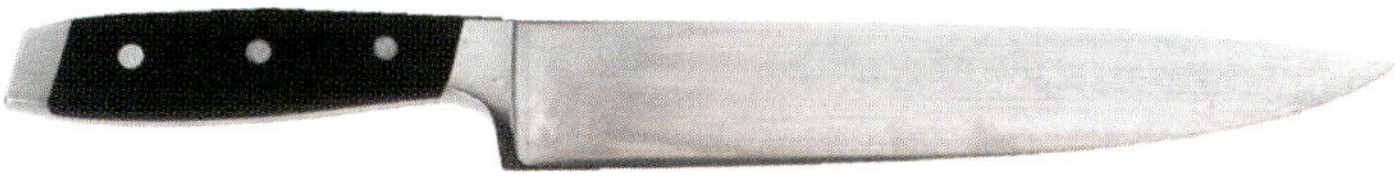

sharp(2)

Tom is **sharp.**
Tom is **quick to understand** things.

shave

I watched father's **shave.**
I watched Father **cut the hair off his face.**

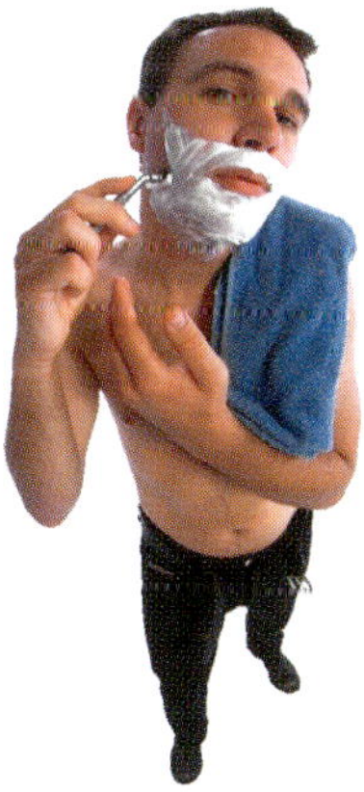

she

A girl is a "**she**".
"**She**" is **not a boy.**

shed(1)

The farmer keeps his tractor in a **shed.**
The **shed** is a low building.

shed(2)
sheds
shedding

Does your dog **shed** his hair?

sheep

A **sheep** is an animal.
A **sheep's** hair is called wool.
A **sheep's** wool is made into cloth.

sheet(1)

Bill is writing on a **sheet** of paper.
Bill is writing on a **piece** of paper.

sheet(2)

I have a **sheet** on my bed.
The **sheet** is nice and smooth.

shelf

The books are on the **shelf.**
The **shelf** is a board fastened to the wall.

shell

An egg **shell** is easy to break.
A nut **shell** is hard to break.
The turtle has a **shell** on its back.

shelter

The house is our **shelter.**

shine(1)
shines
shining
shone

If there are no clouds the moon will **shine** tonight, and the stars will **glimmer.**

shine(2)

I **shine** my shoes every day.
I **polish** my shoes every day.

ship

A **ship** goes across the ocean.
A **ship** is a very large boat.

shirt

John wears a **shirt** under his jacket.
The **shirt** has a collar on it.

shiver

Sometimes when we get cold we **shiver.**
Sometimes when we get cold we **shake.**

shoe

You wear a **shoe** on each foot.
Your **shoes** protect your feet.
Most **shoes** are made of leather but some are made of cloth.

shoot

Hunters **shoot** at wild animals with a gun.

shore

Jack and Jim are playing on the **shore.**

short

Jane is too **short** to reach the book on the shelf.
Jane is **not tall** enough to reach the book.
I have one long pencil and one **short** pencil.

shout

The baby is asleep. Please do not **shout.**

sign(2)

A **sign** tells us something that we should know.
Sometimes a **sign** on the side of the road warns a driver there is danger ahead.
The red **sign** at the corner says, "Stop."

silent

The teacher asked the children to be **silent.**
The teacher asked the children **not** to **make noise.**

silver

Silver is a metal.
Some knives and forks are made of **silver.**

similar

The two houses are **similar.**
The two houses **look alike** but they are not exactly the same.

since

I haven't seen Tom **since** last week.

sing
sings
singing
sang
sung

Mary likes to **sing.**
Yesterday she **sang** three songs.

sister

Betty is Bob's **sister**. Bob is Betty's brother.
They have the same mother and father.

sit
sits
sitting
sat

Bill likes to **sit** in his father's chair.
He **sat** in his father's chair last night.
Bill is **sitting** in his father's chair now.

size

What **size** are your shoes?
How big are your shoes?

skate

Tom is learning to roller **skate.**
Tom **skates** almost every day.
He is **skating** on the sidewalk now.
Tom wears a **skate** on each foot.
Some people like to ice **skate.**

skin

Your body is covered with **skin.**

skip

Ann likes to **skip** the rope.
Ann likes to **jump over** the rope **lightly and quickly**.
Bill's elder brother **skipped** the third grade in school. His brother **passed over** the third grade. He was promoted from the second grade to the fourth grade.

skirt

Jane is wearing a **skirt.** The **skirt** is the part of the dress that hangs from the waist.

sky
skies

The **sky** is the space above the earth.
During the day the **sky** is blue.
Clouds float in the **sky.**

slant

Some houses have roofs that are flat.
Some houses have roofs that **slant.**
When a roof **slants** it is **not flat.**

slap

You should not **slap** your younger brother.
You should not **hit** him **with your open hand.**

sledge

Bill and Tom are on the **sledge.**
The **sledge** is sliding downhill
on the snow.

sleep
sleeps
sleeping
slept

We **sleep** every night.
When we **sleep,**
we are **not awake.**

sleigh

A horse pulls the **sleigh** over the snow.

slice(1)

Would you like a **slice** of bread?
Would you like a **piece** of bread?

slice(2)

My mother will **slice** the bread.
She will **cut** the bread into slices.

slide(1)
slides
sliding
slid

Nancy likes to play on the **slide.**

slide(2)

Watch the girls **slide** down the snowy hill on their sledge.

slip

Be careful on the icy sidewalk or you might **slip.**
Don't let the dish **slip** out of your hand.

slipper

A **slipper** is a low, light shoe.
We wear **slippers** on our feet.

slow

Tom is **slow.**
Tom is **not fast.**
Tom is always **behind time.**

sly

The fox is a **sly** animal.
The fox is a **tricky** animal.

smart

Ann is **smart.**
Ann is **quick to learn** in school.

smell

We **smell** with our nose.
You can tell with your nose if something **smells** good or bad.
Do you like the **smell** of roses?

smile

Bob has a big **smile** on his face.
He **smiles** when he is happy.

smoke(1)

It isn't healthy to **smoke.**

smoke(2)

Smoke is the **grey gas that comes from a fire.**

smooth

The piece of glass is **smooth.**
The piece of glass is **not bumpy.**

snake

A **snake** is a long, thin animal that crawls on the ground.
Some **snakes** crawl in trees. A **snake** has no legs.
Some **snakes**
bite and can hurt you.

sneeze

You should put a handkerchief over your mouth when you **sneeze.**
When you are getting a cold you **sneeze.**
Sometimes pepper will make you **sneeze.**

snow

When rain freezes it turns to **snow.**
The white **snow** falls lightly to the ground.
Did you ever make a **snowman?**

snowflake

The **snowflake** is beautiful.

soap

When we take a bath, we rub **soap** on our body. The **soap** makes the dirt slide off our skin.

sob

Did you hear the baby **sob?**
Did you hear the baby **cry?**
She is **crying softly.**

soft

We sleep on a **soft** pillow.
The pillow is **not hard.**
Jane spoke in a **soft** voice.
Jane spoke in a **mild** voice.

soil(1)

My mother is planting flower seeds in the **soil.**
My mother is planting flower seeds in the **ground.**

soil(2)

Elaine might **soil** her dress.
Elaine might get her dress **dirty.**

some

There are **some** apples left on the tree.
There are **several** apples left on the tree.

son

The mother and the father have a **son.**
The boy is their **son.**

song

Do you know a **song** to sing?
When words and music are put together they make a **song.**
We sang a **song** in school.

soon

Grandmother will visit us **soon.**
Grandmother will visit us **in a short time.**

soprano

A **soprano** is a singer.
When a woman sings in a very high voice we say she is a **soprano.**
My mother sings **soprano.**
My mother sings **very high.**

sorry

I am **sorry** that Mary is sick.
I **feel sad** that Mary is sick.

sort

Ann helped her mother **sort** the clothes.
Ann helped her mother **separate** the clothes.

sound

We hear **sounds** with our ears.
The fire truck makes a loud **sound.**

soup

Do you like **soup?**
Mother makes **soup** by boiling different things in water.
I had **soup** and a sandwich for lunch.

sour

The pickles are **sour.** The pickles are **not sweet.**
Sugar is sweet and lemons are **sour.**

South

South is a direction.
South is toward the bottom part of the earth.
When you face North, **South** is behind you.

sow

The farmer will **sow** corn in the springtime.
The farmer will **plant** corn in the springtime.

space

Is there **space** for one more person in the car?
Is there **room** for one more person in the car?

spade

A **spade** looks like a shovel.
Mother uses a **spade** in her garden.

sparrow

A **sparrow** is a small bird. A **sparrow** is brown and grey.

speak
speaks
speaking
spoke
spoken

I will **speak** to Father about my grades.
I will **talk** to Father about my grades.
A dog cannot **speak**. A dog cannot **say words.**

spectacle

We went to the show in the park.
It was a **spectacle**. There were **many things to see.**
It was a **very large show.**

speed

Speed is how fast or slow something like a car moves.

spell

Can you **spell** your name?
Can you **put the letters in the right order?**

spend
spends
spending
spent

I will **spend** ten cents for popcorn.
I will **pay out** ten cents for popcorn.

spider

A **spider** is a small animal with eight legs.
A **spider** spins a web.

spin

Can you **spin** a top?
Can you **make the top go round and round?**

spinach

Spinach is a green vegetable.
Spinach is a green leaf.
Mother cooks **spinach** for dinner.

square

A **square** has four sides.
All sides of a **square** are of the same size.

squash
squashes

A **squash** is a vegetable.
A **squash** is good to eat.

squeeze

Did you ever **squeeze** an orange?
Did you ever **press hard** to get the juice out of an orange?
I hug my father before going to bed.
I put my arms around his neck and **squeeze** him.

squid

The **squid** is a slender animal
that lives in the sea.
The **squid** has ten arms.
Two of the **squid's** arms
are longer than the other eight.

stable

A **stable** is a building on a farm.
The farmer keeps his cows and horses in the **stable.**

stairs

Ann is going up the **stairs.**
Ann is going up the **steps.**

stake

Joe tied his dog to a **stake.**
Joe tied his dog to a **pole** in the ground.

stalk

Ears of corn grow on a **stalk.**

stamp

You must put a **stamp** on your letter.
The **stamp** is a small piece of paper that shows that you have paid for sending the letter.

star

We see **stars** in the sky at night.
Some of the **stars** are larger than our sun.
The **stars** look very small because they are so far away.

start

The show will **start** at eight o'clock.
The show will **begin** at eight o'clock.

station

A train stops at the railway **station.**
A bus stops at the bus **station.**

stay

Bill will **stay** at home today.
Bill will **not leave** his house.

steal

A person should not **steal** anything.
A person should not **take something that does not belong to him.**

steam

Have you seen **steam** come out of a tea kettle?
When water boils it makes **steam.**

steep

Jack and Jill went up a **steep** hill.

stem

The apple has a **stem** on it.
The **stem** held the apple to the tree.

stick(1)

Tom used a **stick** to bat the ball.
The **stick** is a long thin piece of wood.

stick(2)
sticking
stuck

We **stick** things together with paste.
Please **stick** a stamp on your letter.

stiff

I sat too long in the chair and my leg is **stiff.**
It is difficult to bend it.

still(1)

Is the baby **still** sleeping?

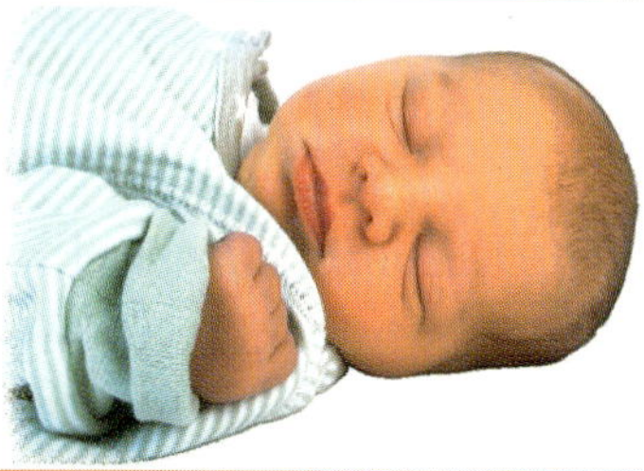

still(2)

The baby is **still.**
The baby is **quiet.**

sting
stings
stinging
stung

Jane is afraid that the bee will **sting**
It hurts when a bee **stings** you.
A **sting** feels like a pin is stuck
in your skin.
Jane was **stung** by a bee once.

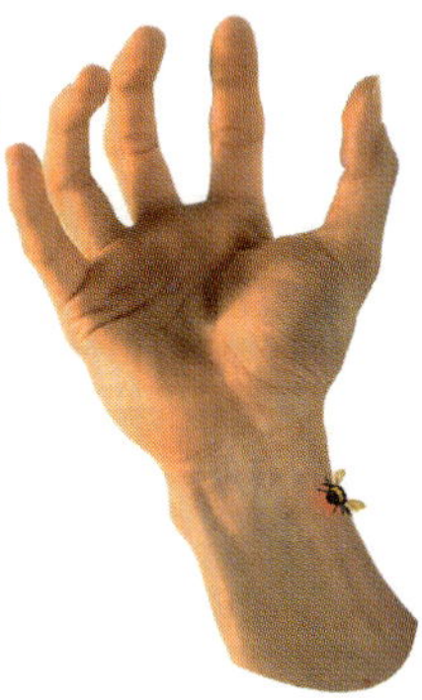

stir

I watched Father **stir** the paint.
I watched Father **mix** the paint.
He moved the paint **round and round** with a stick.

stocking

The **stocking** covers Mary's foot and leg.

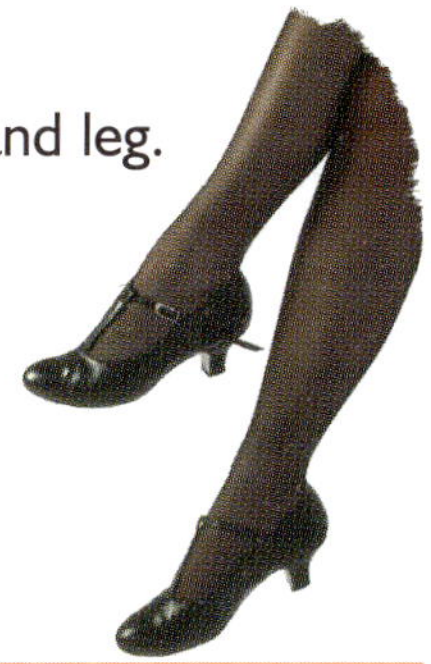

stomach

When you swallow food, it goes into your **stomach**
Your food digests in your **stomach.**

stone

Bill is sitting on a large **stone.**
Bill is sitting on a large **rock.**

stool

A **stool** is a small seat.
The **stool** does not have a back or arms on it.
The farmer sits on a **stool** to milk his cow.

straw(2)

The stem that wheat grows on is called a **straw.**
The **straw** is hollow inside.

stream

Bob is fishing in a **stream** of water.
The **stream** is a small river.

street

You should cross the **street** at the corner.

stretch

The rubber band will **stretch** if you pull it.

strike(1)

The big boy should not **strike** the small boy.
The big boy should not **hit** the small boy.

strike(2)

You should not **strike** matches.

string

A **string** is a long thin cord. The boy uses a **string** to fly the kite. We tie packages with **string.**
The guitar has six **strings** on it.
The guitar **strings** are made of fine wire.

strip

Jane cut a **strip** of paper from the large piece of paper. She cut a **long**, **narrow piece** of paper from the large piece of paper.

stroll

Do you like to **stroll** through the park?
Do you like to **walk in a slow and relaxed way** through the park?

strong

Tom is a **strong** person.
He is **not weak.**
Tom can lift heavy things.

study

Did you **study** your lessons from the book?
Did you **read and try to learn** from the book?

succeed

You must work hard if you want to **succeed.**
You must work hard if you want to **do well.**

such

I have never seen **such** an animal.
I have never seen an animal **like that.**

suddenly

Suddenly it started to rain.
All at once it started to rain.

sugar

My father puts **sugar** in his coffee to make it sweet.

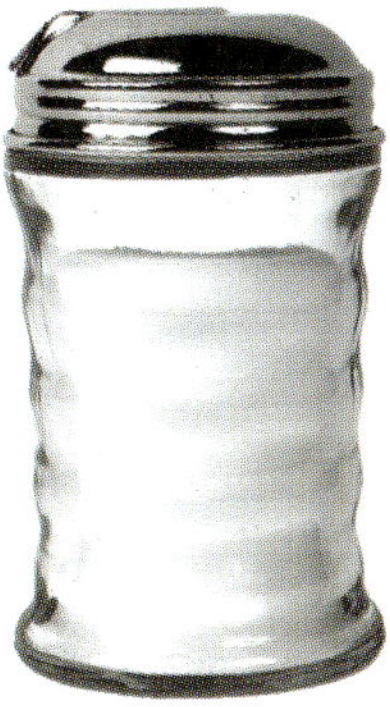

suit(1)

Does that dress **suit** Mary?

suit(2)

Tom is wearing a new **suit.** He is wearing a **coat and pant that match.**

summer

Summer is one of the four seasons in a year.
Summer is the warmest time of the year.

sun

The **sun** shines in the daytime.
The **sun** makes things warm.
The **sun** helps make things grow.

supper

Supper is our last meal of the day.
We eat **supper** in the evening.

suppose

Do you **suppose** it will rain today?
Do you **think** it will rain today?

sure
surer
surest

I am **sure** Joan's new dress is red and white.
I **know** Joan's new dress is red and white.

surprise

Mother brought home a gift to **surprise** me.
I **did not expect** a gift. It was a nice **surprise.**

swallow(1)

You must chew your food before you **swallow** it. You must chew your food before it **goes down your throat into your stomach.**

swallow(2)

Swallow is the name of a bird.

sweater

Jane's mother knitted her a **sweater.** She made the **sweater** out of yarn. Jane will wear the **sweater** on the upper part of her body to keep warm.

sweep
sweeps
sweeping
swept

Mary is helping **sweep** the floor. She is using a broom to **sweep** the dirt and dust up.

table

A **table** is a piece of furniture. We sit at a **table** when we have dinner. The **table** has a flat top held up by legs.

tag

Did you ever play **tag?**
When you play **tag,** you must **tag** another boy or girl.
You must **touch** another boy or girl.

tail

When a dog is happy he wags his **tail.** Most animals have a **tail.**
A rabbit has a short **tail.** A cat has a long **tail.**

tailor

A **tailor** is a person who can sew.
A **tailor** can make new clothes.
A **tailor** can mend clothes that are torn.

take

takes
taking
took
taken

Jane will **take** all of her books home.
Bill's father will **take** him to the ball game.
Bill's father will **go with** him to the ball game.

tale

Mother read us a **tale** about the Three Bears.

talk

When we **talk,** we say something.
Bill likes to **talk** with Betty.

tall
taller
tallest

John is **tall**
Jane is **short.**
John is **taller** than Jane.

tangle

Sometimes when you sleep your hair will get **tangled.**
When your hair is **tangled,** it is hard to comb.

tank

A **tank** is a large container used to hold liquid.
Our car has a gas **tank.**

tap (1)

Did you hear a **tap** on the door?
Did you hear a **light knock** at the door?

tap (2)

Water runs out of the **tap** into the sink.

task

A **task** is a **special job** we must do.
My **task** is to make my bed each morning.

taste

I like the **taste** of lemonade.

tea

Sometimes my mother makes **tea.**
She pours hot water over dried **tea** leaves.
My mother takes **tea.** I drink milk.

teach
teaches teaching taught

John will **teach** the dog to roll over.
John will **help** the dog **learn** how to roll over.
John **taught** the dog how to catch a ball in its mouth.

teacher

Our **teacher** helps us to learn things.
The **teacher** will teach us how to read.

team

The boys have a baseball **team.**
Mary plays on the basketball **team.**

tear (1)

tears
tearing
tore
torn

Ann did not want to **tear** her dress.
Ann did not want to **make a hole** in her dress.
She **tore** her dress on the fence.
The dress is **torn** and she is sorry.

tear (2)

The baby has **tears** on her face.
The **tears** are **small drops of water** that came out of her eyes.

teaspoon

A **teaspoon** is a small spoon.
I take ice cream with a **teaspoon.**

tedious

This job is **tedious.** This job is **boring.**

telephone

Jane is talking to Bill over the **telephone.** Jane's voice is going through a wire to Bill's **telephone.**

tell
tells
telling
told

Bob will not **tell** where he has been.
Bob will not **say** where he has been.

ten

Ten is a number.
Betty's eder brother is **ten** years old.
When we count to **ten** we say:
1, 2, 3, 4, 5, 6, 7, 8, 9, **10.**

tender

This meat is **tender.** This meat is **not tough.**

tend

Mary **tends** the baby. Mary **takes care** of the baby.

tent

Bob and Bill slept in a **tent.**
The **tent** is like a **house made of cloth.**
We saw the circus in a big **tent.**

terrible

We had a **terrible** storm today.
The storm made everyone afraid.
Nancy has a **terrible** cold.
Nancy has a **very bad** cold.

test

The teacher gave a spelling **test.**

than

John is bigger **than** Jack.
John can run faster **than** Jack.

thank

When someone gives you something you say, "**Thank** you."
Bill opened the door for the lady.
The lady said, "**Thank** you."

that

This is my coat and **that** is your coat.

their

The birds are in **their** nest.
The birds are in the nest that **belongs to them.**
The birds are waiting for **their** mother.

then

Ann ate her lunch and **then** went to play.
Ann ate her lunch and **afterwards** went to play.

there

Please wait **there** until I return.
Please wait **in that place** until I return.

they

Betty, Ann and Joe are playing.
They are having fun.
Our team played baseball and **they** won.

thick

This is a **thick** book.
This book is **not thin.**

thief

A person who takes things which do not belong to him is called a **thief.**
A **thief** is a person who steals things.

thimble

Mother puts a **thimble** on the end of her finger when she sews.
She pushes the needle through the cloth with the **thimble.**
The **thimble** keeps the needle from sticking her finger.

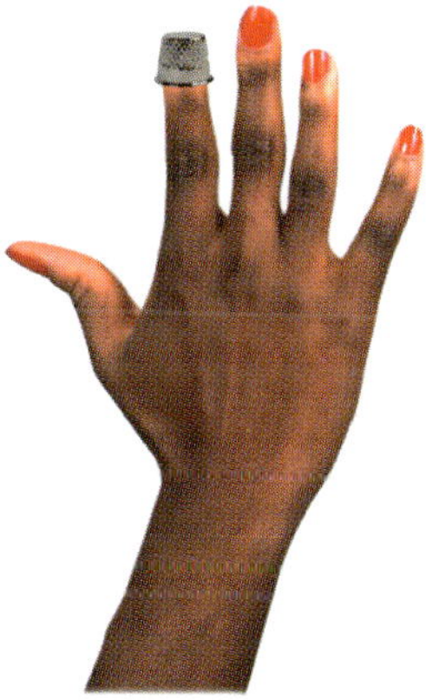

thin
thinner
thinnest

When something is **thin** it is **not thick.**
A page in this book is **thin.** The book is thick.
Caroline is **thin.** She is **not fat.**

thing

John is writing on the sidewalk. That is a bad **thing** to do.
The next **thing** he should do is to clean the sidewalk.

think

I **think** it will rain today.
I **believe** it will rain today.

this

That book is yours, but **this** book is mine. **This** is my house.
We must go to school **this** morning.

thorns

Thorns grow on some plants.
A rose bush has **thorns** on it.
A **thorn** has a **sharp point that can stick** into your finger.

those

These flowers are mine but **those** flowers are my mother's.
Those flowers are in mother's flower garden.

though

Jane came to the party even **though** it was late.
It was late but she came anyway.

thread

Mother sews clothes with **thread.**
Thread is a **very fine string.**

throat

Betty is holding her **throat.**
Betty is holding the **front part of her neck.**
Betty has a sore **throat.**

throne

A king and queen sit on a **throne.**
The **throne** is a **chair** where the king or queen sits.

through

We rode **through** a tunnel in the mountain.
We rode from one side of the mountain to the other side **through** the tunnel.

throw
throws
throwing
threw
thrown

Jack likes to **throw** the basketball.

thunder

Sometimes when it rains we see lightning and hear **thunder.**
The **thunder** makes a loud noise.

tick

The sound a clock or watch makes is called a **tick.**

tickle

When I go barefoot the grass makes my foot **tickle.**

tidy
tidier
tidiest

Mary keeps her room **tidy.** It is **neat and clean.**
John does not keep his room un**tidy.** It is **neat and clean.**

tie (1)
ties
tying
tied

Bill can **tie** his shoelaces.
Bill knows how to **make a knot** in the shoelace.

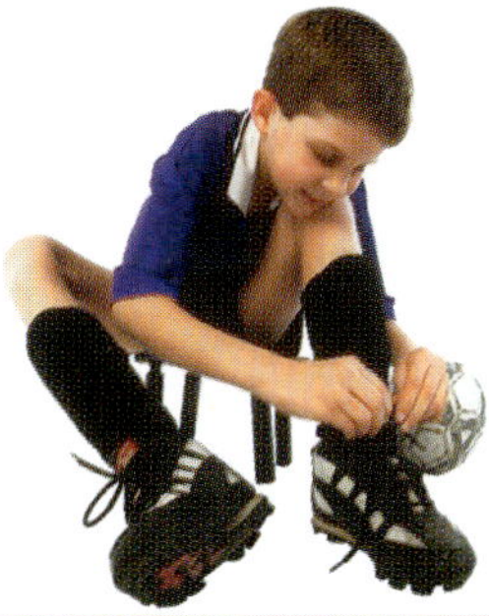

tie (2)

My father wears a **tie.** The **tie** is made of cloth.

tiger

The **tiger** is a wild **animal.**
The **tiger** is a **large cat.**
The **tiger's** fur has black stripes.

till

Mary slept **till** nine o'clock.

time

Can you tell **time?**
Can you look at a clock and tell what **time** it is?

tin

Tin is a **metal.**
Some cans are made of **tin.**

tiny
tinier
tiniest

A **tiny** bird fell out of the nest. It was **very little.**

tip (1)

You shouldn't stand up in the boat. It might **tip** over.
It might **turn** over.

tip (2)

The **tip** of the pencil is sharp.

tyre

The car has a flat **tyre.**
The **tyre** is made of rubber.
There is a **tyre** on each wheel of a car.

tired

Jim worked hard
and he is **tired.**
He is **tired** and
now he will rest.

title

Do you know the **title** of this book?
Do you know the **name** of this book?

toad

A **toad** is an animal that looks like a frog.
A **toad** lives on the land.
The **toad** eats bugs and worms.

toast

My mother makes **toast** for breakfast.

today

Today is Ann's birthday.
This day is Ann's birthday.

touch

Don't **touch** the dog. It might bite you.
Don't **put your hand on** the dog.

tough

This guava is **tough.**
This guava is **not soft.**
This guava is **hard** to chew.

toward

Betty is walking **towards** the school.
Betty is walking **in the direction of** the school.
She will be at the school in a short time.

towel

A **towel** is a piece of cloth or soft paper.
We dry things with a **towel.**
Mother dries dishes with a dish **towel.**
We have **towels** in the bathroom.

toy

Jane has a **toy** watch.
It is **not** a **real** watch.
A **toy** is something to play with.

track(1)

The train runs on a railway **track.**
The **track** is made of two iron rails.

track(2)

Animals make **tracks** in the snow.

trade

I will **trade** papers with you.
If you give me your paper I **will give** you my paper.

traffic

There is too much **traffic** in this street.
There are too many **cars and trucks that go by.**

train(1)

Tom is trying to **train** his dog.
Tom is trying to **teach his dog to obey** him.

train(2)

A row of railway coaches pulled by an engine is called a **train.**

tramp(1)

My mother said, "Don't **tramp** in the mud."
My mother said, "Don't **walk** in the mud."

tramp(2)

A person that has no home and walks from town to town is called a **tramp.**

trap

A **trap** is used to catch animals.
This is a mouse **trap.**

This is a bear **trap.**

travel

When we **travel** we **go from one place to another.**
I like to **travel** in the car. I like to **go** in the car.
Some people **travel** in the train. Some people **travel** in an airplane.

tray

The waiter brought our food on a **tray.**

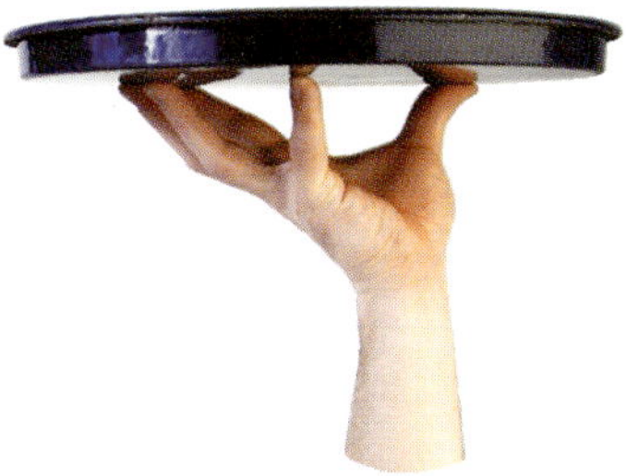

treat

You should **treat** your dog well.
You should **act** well **towards** your dog.

tree

A **tree** is a tall plant.
There are many kinds of **trees.**
Some **trees** lose their leaves when the weather gets cold.
A pine **tree** stays green the whole year.

trial

Jim gave his new bike a **trial** to see how it rides.
The teacher gave John another **trial.**
The teacher gave John another **chance.**

tricycle

The **tricycle** has three wheels.
Bill has a bicycle and his younger brother has a **tricycle.**

trim

The barber will **trim** my hair.
The barber will **cut a little bit** off my hair.

trip(1)

We go on a **trip** every year.
We go on a **journey** every year.

trip(2)

Bob **tripped** in the rope and fell.
Bob got his foot **caught** in the rope and fell.

trouble

It isn't any **trouble** to bring you the book.
It isn't any **extra work** to bring you the book.

trousers

Tom spilled ink on his **trousers.**

truck

A **truck** is used to carry things in.
There are many different kinds of **trucks.**
A fire **truck** carries things to put out a fire.
The dump **truck** carries dirt and rocks.

true
truer
truest

The story Mary told was **true.**

The story Mary told was **not false.**

The story was **not a lie.**

trunk(1)

The main stem of a tree is called a **trunk.** The part of a person's body from the top of the legs to the neck is called a **trunk.**

trunk(2)

Mother puts clothes in a **trunk.**
The **trunk** is a **large box** with a lid on it.

trunk(3)

The elephant's nose is his **trunk**.

trust

Dorothy tells the truth and I **trust** her. Dorothy tells the truth and I **believe** her. You can **trust** a person who is honest.

try

Bill will **try** hard to win the race.
Bill will **do his best** to win the race.

tube

The hose that we water the grass with is a **tube**.
The pipe that brings water into the house is a **tube**.
Tube of the car is made of rubber.
Toothpaste comes in a **tube**.
Glue comes in a **tube**.

tulip

A **tulip** is a flower.
The **tulip** has a beautiful, bright colour.

turkey

A **turkey** is a large bird.
A **turkey** is good to eat.

turn

When you ride a bike the wheels **turn**.
The wheels go **round and round**.
Father will **turn** at the next corner.
Father will **change directions** at the next corner.

turtle

A **turtle** has a shell on its back.
The **turtle** has four legs but walks very slowly.
A **turtle** lives on the land and in the water.

tusk

A **tusk** is a long tooth. An elephant has two **tusks** that stick out of his mouth. Some other animals have **tusks** too.

twin

Bill and Bob are **twins.** Bill and Bob are brothers who were born on the same day.

twinkle

Stars **twinkle** at night. The stars **sparkle** at night.

twist

Twist means to turn something.
Did you **twist** the rope?

ugly
uglier
ugliest

The witch in the movie was **ugly.** She was **not nice to look at.** When the witch spoke she sounded **ugly.** She sounded **angry and mean.**

umbrella

Mary is walking in the rain. She is holding an **umbrella** over her head. Mary will stay dry underneath the **umbrella.**

uncertain

Tom thinks he knows the answer but he is **uncertain.** Tom thinks he knows the answer but he is **not sure.**

uncle

My father's brother is my **uncle.**
My mother's brother is my **uncle.**
My aunt's husband is my **uncle.**

under

The cat is asleep **under** the chair.
The cat is asleep **beneath** the chair.

uneasy

Does a bad storm make you **uneasy?**
Does a bad storm make you **uncomfortable?**
Does a bad storm make you **worry?**

unhappy

The rain made Jack **unhappy.**
The rain made Jack **sad.**
He wanted to go out and play.

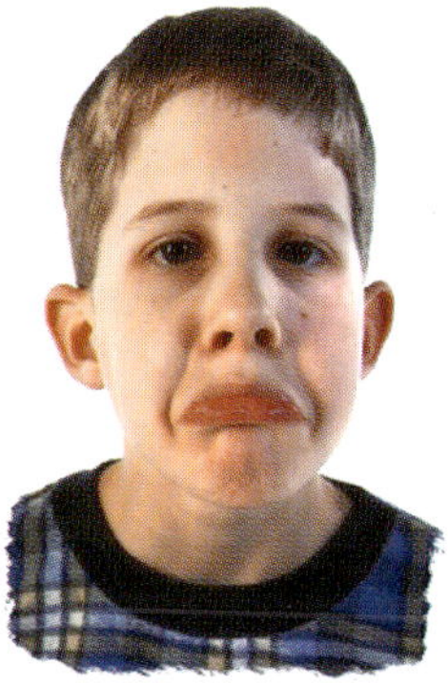

unkind

Tom was **unkind** to his dog.
Tom was **not kind** to his dog.

unless

You need not come with me **unless** you want to.
You need not come with me if you do not want to.

untie

John tied the dog to a tree with a rope. Now he must **untie** the knot. Now he must **open up** the knot and let the dog loose.

upon

We saw the cat **upon** our roof. We saw the cat **on** our roof.

use

We **use** our hand to hold things. We **use** our mind to think with. I **use** a pencil to write with.

useful

My raincoat is **useful.** My raincoat keeps me dry. This book is **useful.** This book helps me to learn things. Tools are **useful.** Tools help us to build things.

vacant

The house next door is **vacant.** The house next door is **empty.**
Next to the **vacant** house is a **vacant** plot.
The **vacant** plot is a piece of land that **does not have a building on it.**

vacation

My father will take a **vacation** next summer. My father will **stay away from work** for sometime. Sometimes we take a trip when my father has his **vacation.** We go to the country to take **rest.**

valley

A **valley** is **the land between hills.** A river runs through the **valley.**

value

What is the **value** of the bike? What is the **price** of the bike?
How much is the bike **worth?**

vase

Mother puts flowers in a **vase.**
The **vase** looks like a tall bowl.

vegetable

A **vegetable** is a plant. We eat **vegetables** with our food. **Vegetables** are good for your health. Carrots, peas, cabbage and potatoes are **vegetables.**

verse

Mary remembers one **verse** of the poem.
Mary remembers **one line** of the poem.

very

That is a **very** large dog.
That is an **extra** large dog.

view

The picture shows a beautiful **view** of the mountains.
The picture shows a beautiful **scene** of the mountains.

village

A small group of houses is called a **village.**
We have one store in our **village.**
A **village** is smaller than a town.

vine

A **vine** is a plant that grows along the ground or up a wall.
We gather grapes from a **vine.**
Grapes grow on a **vine.**

violin

A **violin** is a musical instrument.
John is learning to play the **violin.**

visit

Do you like to **visit** your grandmother?
Do you like to **go and see** your grandmother?

voice

The sound that you make with your throat and mouth is your **voice.**
When we talk we use our **voice.**
Mary likes to sing because she has a good **voice.**

vote

The boys will select a president for their club.
Each boy will **vote** for the person he wants to be president.
The boy who gets the most **votes** will be president.

wade

Do you like to **wade** the water?
Do you like to **walk** in the water?

wag

See the dog **wag** his tail.
See the dog **move** his tail **from side to side.**
The dog **wags** his tail when he is happy.

wagon

John is giving Jane a ride in his **wagon.**
The **wagon** has four wheels and a handle to pull it by.

wait

I will **wait** here until you return.
I will **stay** here until you return.

wake

If you make too much noise you will **wake** up the baby.
If you make too much noise the baby will **stop sleeping.**

walk

Some children ride the bus to school.
Some children **walk** to school.
Some children **go on** their own **feet.**

wall

We have a rock **wall** around the yard.
The **wall** keeps the dogs in the yard.
The side of the house is called a **wall.**
I have a picture hanging on the **wall** of my room.

want

Do you **want** some of the cake?
Would you **like to have** some of the cake?

warm

The cat likes a glass of **warm** milk.
The milk **isn't hot and it isn't cold.**
The milk is **warm.**

warn

The teacher said, "I must **warn** you to be quiet."
The teacher said, "I must **tell** you **ahead of time** to be quiet."

wash

Betty is going to **wash** the baby.
Betty is going to **bathe** the baby.

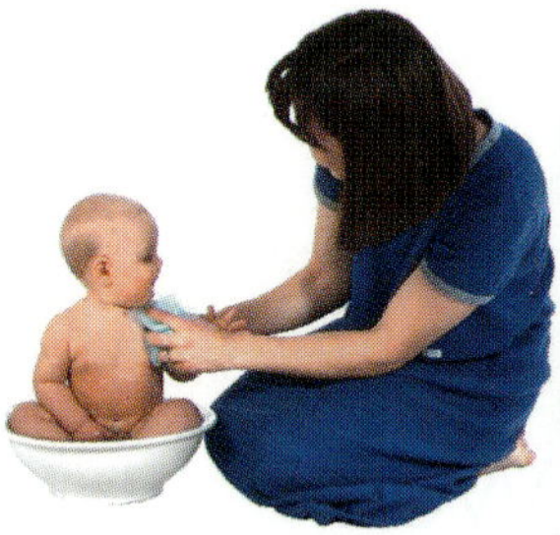

waste

You should not **waste** food.
Throw this **waste** in a dustbin.

watch (1)

Jane will **watch** the baby for her mother.
Jane will **look after** the baby for her mother.

watch (2)
watches

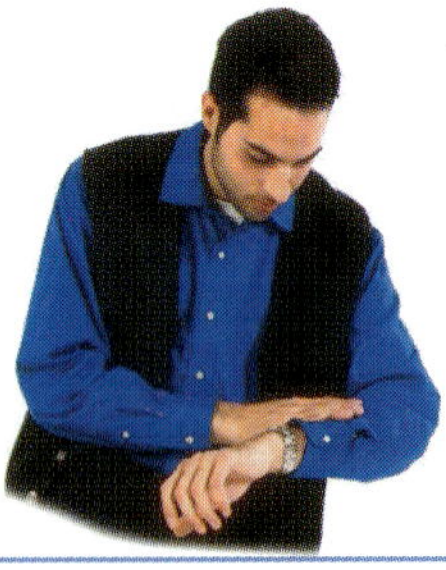

Tom is wearing a new **watch** on his wrist.
The **watch** tells him what time it is.

water (1)

Water is a liquid.
When we are thirsty we drink **water.**
Most of our earth is covered with **water.**

water (2)

My father will **water** the lawn today.
My father will **put water on** the lawn today.

wave

We saw a large **wave** in the ocean.
The **wave** was like a **mountain of water.**

way

You must show me the **way** to your house.
You must show me **how to get to** your house.

weak

Mary has been sick and she is **weak.**
Mary has been sick and she is **not strong.**

wear

wears
wearing
wore
worn

John likes to **wear** his new suit.
John **is dressed** in his new suit.
John **wore** the suit yesterday.
He put the suit this morning and he is **wearing** it now.

weary

wearier
weariest

Mother worked all day and she is **weary.**
Mother worked all day and she is **tired.**

weather

We are having cold **weather** today.
The **air outdoors** is cold.
Yesterday we had warm **weather.**
Sometimes we have rainy **weather.**

weed

A **weed** is a plant that grows where it isn't wanted.
The **dandelion** is a **weed.**

week

There are seven days in a **week.**
The days in a **week** are Sunday, Monday, Tuesday, Wednesday, Thursday, Friday and Saturday. There are fifty-two **weeks** in a year.

weep
weeps
weeping
wept

Jane hurt her knee and she started to **weep.**
Jane hurt her knee and she started to **cry.**
She **wept** for a short time.

weigh

We **weigh** ourselves to see **how heavy we are.**
Last year I weighed forty pounds. Now I **weigh** fifty pounds.

wet
wetter
wettest

Bob was in the rain and his clothes are **wet.**
Bob was in the rain and his clothes are **not dry.**

whale

The **whale** is a large animal that lives in the sea. Some **whales** are larger than any other kind of animal.

what

What is that thing in the pond?
Do you know **what** it is?

wheel

A **wheel** is round.
A bike has two **wheels.**
A wagon has four **wheels.**
When the **wheels** turn the wagon moves.

when

When are you going to school?
At what time are you going to school?

which

Which way are you going home?

while

You shouldn't watch television **while** you read.
You shouldn't watch television **at the same time** as you read.

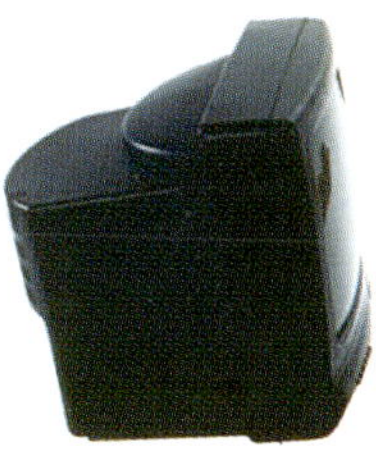

whip

Jack does not **whip** his dog.
Jack does not **hit** his dog.

whistle (I)

Can you **whistle?**
Can you **blow air through your lips and make a loud sound?**

whistle (2)

The policeman at the corner has a **whistle.**
Some trains have a **whistle.**

who

Do you know **who** won the race?
I can tell you **who** he is.

whole

John ate the **whole** pie.
John ate **all of** the pie.
This is a **whole** apple.
This apple is **not cut apart.**

whose

Whose coat is this? Is it yours?

why

Do you know **why** the baby is crying?
Do you know **the reason** the baby is crying?

wide

wider
widest

This is a **wide** street.
This street is **not narrow.**

wild

The lion is a **wild** animal.
The lion is **not** a **tame** animal.

win
wins
winning
won

Bill and Tom are running a race to the tree.
I think Tom will **win** the race.
I think Tom will **get to the tree first.**

wind (1)

I **wind** my watch every day.

wind (2)

The **wind** is blowing hard. The **air** is **moving fast.**
When the **wind** moves slowly we call it a breeze.
When the **wind** blows very hard we call it a **windstorm.**

windmill

The **windmill** pumps water out of the ground.
The wind makes the **windmill** turn.

window

The **window** is made of glass.
I have two **windows** in my room.
I can see through the **window.**
We open the **window** to let fresh air in.

wing

The **wings** of birds are covered with feathers.
Birds fly with two **wings.**
An airplane has two **wings.**
The **wings** of an airplane hold it up in the air.
My father built a **wing** on the house.
My father built **an extra room** on the house.

winsome

Mary is a **winsome** girl.
Mary is a **pretty and pleasant** girl.

winter

The four seasons of the year are **winter,** spring, summer and autumn.
Summer is the warm season and **winter** is the cold season. I ride my sledge in the **winter.**

wipe

After we take a bath, we **wipe** our body with a towel.
We **rub** our body with a towel to dry the water off.

wire

A **wire** is a long **thin piece of metal that will bend.** A **wire** is like a metal rope. Some fences are made of **wire.** When we telephone someone our voices go through the telephone **wire.**

wise
wiser
wisest

I think father is very **wise.**
I think father is very **clever.**

wish (I)
wishes

Jane blew the candles out and she made a **wish.**
Jane blew the candles out and she **asked for something she wanted most of all.**

wish (2)

I **wished** that Grandmother would visit us.
I **hoped** that Grandmother would visit us.

witch
witches

The teacher read us a story about a **witch.** The **witch** was a mean old woman. The **witch** could do magic tricks. **Witches** are not real. **Witches** are make-believe.

with

We live **with** our mother and father. We live **together.** You see **with** your eyes. You **use** your eyes to see. John is standing **with** the dog. John is standing **by the side of** the dog.

witness
witnesses

I did not spill the milk. John is my **witness.** John **saw** exactly **what happened.** The cat spilled the milk.

wolf
wolves

The **wolf** is a wild animal. The **wolf** looks like a large dog. A **wolf** eats meat.

woman
women

My mother is a **woman.**
My father is a man.
Mary is a girl. She will grow up into a **woman.**

wood

We make things with **wood.**
We cut down trees to get **wood.**
The table is made of **wood.**

woods

Sometimes we walk in the **woods.**
Sometimes we walk in the **jungle.**

wool

The hair on a sheep is called **wool. Wool** is made into cloth. **Wool** clothes keep us warm.

word

You should learn every **word** in this book. When we talk we say **words.** When we write we write **words.** A **word** is part of a sentence.

work

Jane likes to **work** in the garden. Jane finished her **work** and now she will rest. Bob's new toy does not **work.** Bob's new toy does not **do what it should do.** My father goes to **work** five days a week. My father goes to **his job** five days a week.

world

All of us live in one **world.** Our earth and sky is our **world.** Our **world** is round.

worm

A **worm** is a long, thin insect that crawls. Some **worms** live in the ground and some **worms** live in trees. Birds like to eat **worms.**

worry

If you don't come home on time, your mother will **worry.** If you don't come home on time, your mother will **think something bad could have happened to you.**

worse
bad
worst

Jack has been sick. He is **worse** today.
Joan sings **worse** than Mary.

worth

This book is **worth** one dollar. The book **costs** one dollar.

wrap

Before Bill gives Ann the gift, he will **wrap** it.
He will **cover the gift with paper** and tie it with a ribbon.
When Bill gave Ann the gift, she **wrapped** her arms around him.

wring

Caroline has been swimming.
Now she will **wring** out her bathing suit.
She will **twist** the bathing suit until most of the water is out.

---

write
writes
writing
wrote
written

John likes to **write** on the blackboard.
John likes to **put words and letters** on the blackboard.
He **wrote** his name on the blackboard.
John thinks **writing** is fun.
He has **written** all over the blackboard.

---

wrong

What is **wrong** with the light? It won't turn on.
What is **the problem** with the light?
Jack spelled ten words right and two **wrong.**
Jack spelled ten words right and two **not right.**
It is **wrong** to tell a lie. It is **not the right thing** to do.

x-ray

Sometimes the doctor will take **x-rays** of your body.
The **x-ray** machine is like a camera.
The **x-ray** machine takes pictures through your skin and into the inside of your body.
The **x-ray** will show if there is anything wrong with you.

xylophone

The **xylophone** is a musical instrument.
The **xylophone** has rows of wooden bars
Each bar makes a different sound when it is hit by a small wooden hammer.

yard

The children are playing in the **yard.**
The children are playing on the **ground around the house.**

yarn

Yarn is like a heavy string.
Yarn can be made from wool, cotton or silk.
I have a sweater made of **yarn.**

yawn

When we are sleepy we **yawn.**
We **open our mouth and take a deep breath.**

year

A **year** is a **measure of time.** There are twelve months in a **year.**
Joan's baby sister is one **year** old.
We have a birthday every **year.**

yell

You should not **yell** at your sister.
You should not **shout** at your sister.
You should not **cry out loudly** at your sister.

yellow

Yellow is a **colour.** The banana is **yellow.**
A dandelion is **yellow.**

yes

When you say **"yes"**, it means you **agree** to something.
When you say "no" it means you do not agree.

yet

Bill will be here but he has not **yet** come.
Bill will be here but he has not come **up till now.**
It did not rain but there is **yet** a chance of rain.
It did not rain but there is **still** a chance of rain.
Don't eat your dessert **so soon.**

you

Does this pencil belong to **you?**
You are the person I am speaking to.

young

Mary is too **young** to drink tea.
Mary is **not old** enough to drink tea.

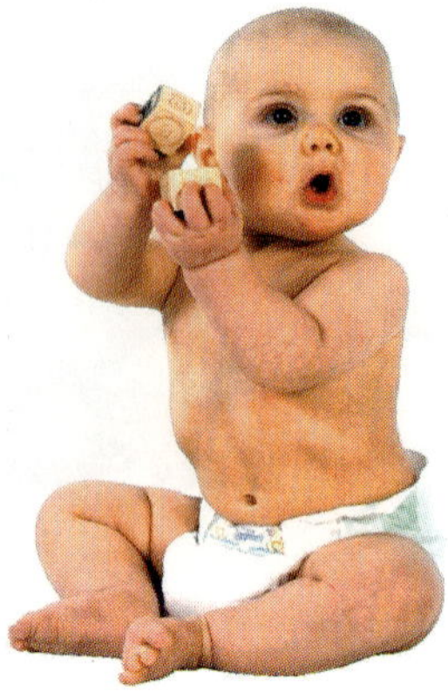

your

Is that **your** dog?

zebra

A **zebra** is an animal that lives in Africa.
A **zebra** has dark and white stripes on its body.
The **zebra** looks like a small striped horse.

zero

Zero means **nothing.** The teacher put a **zero** on Bill's paper. All of Bill's answers were wrong. Father said, "It's almost **zero** outside." Father said, "It's **very, very cold** outside." This is a **zero: 0.**

zone

A city is divided into different parts. We call each part a **zone.**

zoo

People catch wild animals and put them in the **zoo.**
We go to the **zoo** to see the animals.